Contents

Preface

Economic growth features in the new subject criteria for A level Economics – and hence the new A level specifications – and is a key topic on HND and degree courses. Owing to a global crisis, economic growth – and in particular fluctuations in economic activity – has recently made its way on to the front pages of newspapers and has even been the leading feature on TV and radio news broadcasts.

In writing this book I have sought to discuss the main issues involved in economic growth and *business cycles*. These include a number of unresolved issues, such as what is the prime determinant of economic growth and which policies are the most effective in promoting stable and sustainable growth.

Economic growth is a crucial area of economics. It affects everyone's life. I hope this book manages to capture at least some of its importance and fascination.

Susan Grant
Series Editor

Introduction

Roy Harrod wrote, in 1965, 'Economic growth is the grand objective. It is the aim of economic policy as a whole.' Economic growth can bring with it significant improvements in living standards. However, depending on how it is achieved it may also bring disadvantages.

For centuries economists have sought to understand how economic growth occurs and why there are periodic fluctuations in growth. The causes of economic growth was indeed the main topic of one of the most famous economic books ever written – *An Inquiry Into the Nature and Causes of the Wealth of Nations* by Adam Smith, published in 1776. In more recent times ground-breaking work has been undertaken on economic growth and business cycles by, for example, Robert Solow of the Massachusetts Institute of Technology (MIT) and Robert Lucas of the University of Chicago.

This book seeks to explore the meaning of economic growth and business cycles, their causes, consequences and implications for government and international policy.

Chapter 1 defines economic growth and distinguishes between actual and potential growth. The difference between real and nominal gross domestic product (GDP) is explained, and the output gap and sustainable growth are discussed.

Chapter 2 explores the causes of economic growth. A distinction is made, using aggregate demand and supply analysis, between the short-run and long-run causes.

Chapter 3 considers the causes in more depth by examining what are considered to be the key determinants of economic growth and growth theories, including the Harrod–Domar model, Rostow's theory and Lewis's model, the new classical and new growth theories.

Chapter 4 is concerned with comparing economic growth rates over time and between countries. It starts by discussing the problems involved in the measurement and interpretation of GDP figures. The causes of differences in growth rate figures are examined, and attention is paid to the relatively slow growth of the UK economy and the difficulties some developing countries experience in seeking to raise their growth rates.

Chapter 5 discusses the benefits and costs of economic growth, including higher living standards and the depletion of non-renewable resources.

Chapter 6 explores the relationship between government policy and economic growth. Government objectives in relation to growth and possible policy measures are discussed.

Chapter 7 looks at the interrelationships between economic growth and the five key markets of housing, health, education, tourism and information technology.

Chapter 8 moves our attention towards examining fluctuations in economic growth in the form of business cycles. The phases of a business cycle are explained and different types of business cycle are discussed. Then the explanations of business cycles are explored.

Chapter 9 examines the recent global financial crisis which has seen a number of countries with previously high growth rates move into recession.

Chapter 10 is about forecasting economic growth, including the reasons for doing it, the indicators used and the degree of accuracy to be expected.

Chapter One

The meaning and measurement of economic growth

'Growth in the productive capacity of a developed economy is inevitable'
W. Eltis

Definition

Economic growth is an increase in the output of a country's goods and services. It is usually measured by changes in real gross domestic product (GDP). So, for example, a growth rate of 3 per cent means that real GDP is 3 per cent higher this year then the previous year and more goods and services have been produced.

Figure 1 shows the UK's growth rate over about two decades up to 1998. Real GDP grew by *an average* of 2.2 per cent. However, for most of the period the rate of growth was not very steady. Relatively high increases in GDP were experienced in, for example, 1978, 1987 and 1988. In 1980 and 1981, and again in 1991 and 1992, there was actually negative growth. This means that in 1991 the UK produced less than in 1990, and in 1992 output fell again. When output declines

Figure 1 Gross domestic product at constant prices, 1977–98

3

over a period of more than six months the situation is referred to as a **recession**. So as Figure 1 shows, the UK experienced recessions in 1980/81 and 1991/92.

Nominal and real GDP

Governments calculate gross domestic product in both nominal and real terms.

- **Nominal GDP** is also referred to as 'money GDP' or 'GDP in current prices'. As these names suggest, this is gross domestic product measured in terms of the prices operating in the year in question.
- **Real GDP** or 'GDP in constant prices' is gross domestic product measured in terms of the prices operating in a given base year. It is GDP adjusted for inflation.

It is important to make an adjustment for inflation as otherwise a misleading impression could be gained about what is happening to a country's output. For example, if GDP were initially £100 billion and then the general price level rose by 10 per cent, nominal GDP would increase by 10 per cent even if output had not changed.

Table 1 shows nominal GDP increasing at a more rapid rate than real GDP for the two years and for the 20-year period given. This will be true whenever the general price level is rising – that is, whenever there is inflation. If the nominal figure were to be used to assess economic growth it would give the impression that output had risen by nearly 9 per cent annually from 1977 to 1997. This would be incorrect as the figure is an inflated one. *So in assessing economic growth the emphasis is placed on changes in real GDP as these are caused solely by changes in output and not by changes in the general price level.*

Table 1 Comparison of real and nominal GDP changes

	Percentage change in real GDP	*Percentage change in nominal GDP*
1996	2.6	5.9
1997	3.5	6.3
1977–97	2.2	8.9

Source: ONS, National Income Accounts, *The Blue Book,* 1998

Actual and potential growth

A country can increase its output either by making more and better use of existing resources or by increasing the quantity or quality of its resources.

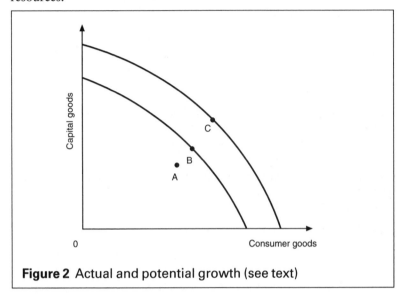

Figure 2 Actual and potential growth (see text)

Figure 2 shows output increasing from point A to point B as the economy employs previously unemployed resources. It also shows output rising from point B to point C as a result of, for example, an increase in the labour force.

Whereas **actual growth** occurs when the country produces more goods and services, **potential growth** arises when a country's

---

PRODUCTION AND PRODUCTIVITY

Production is the output of goods and services, whereas *productivity* is output per factor of production. Labour productivity may be measured as output per worker or, to take account of part-time workers, output per hour worked. Rises in productivity mean that an economy is operating more efficiently.

So a rise in production may be the result of an increase in, for example, the number of workers employed or a rise in the productivity of workers. It would be possible, given productivity increases, for production to rise with a smaller workforce.

productive potential increases. It results from a rise in the quantity and/or quality of resources. The shift outwards of the production possibility curve illustrates potential growth.

Actual and potential growth can coincide if a country is initially producing at its maximum **productive capacity** and then the next year its output rises in line with any increase in productive capacity. This is illustrated by the movement from point B to point C in Figure 2.

The output gap
In practice actual growth does not often match potential growth. A country may, for example, be experiencing an **output gap**. This occurs when the output of a country is below its potential output i.e. it is producing within its production possibility curve. In this case if its actual output increases at a greater rate than its potential output, its output gap will be reduced. Figure 3 shows a country's output gap narrowing. Whereas if its actual growth is below its potential growth, the output gap will widen.

Overheating
There may be occasions when *aggregate demand* is increasing at a more rapid rate than the productive potential. This is sometimes referred to as an economy **overheating**. It is a situation which cannot be sustained for long. It is also a situation which a government is unlikely to tolerate.

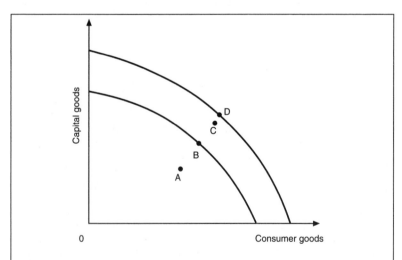

Figure 3 The output gap narrowing: the initial output gap is AB; then, over time, the gap narrows to CD

This is because it will pose the risk that *demand-pull inflation* and a *balance of payments deficit* may arise.

Trend growth

Trend growth refers to the expected increase in the productive capacity of a country – its expected potential growth which occurs over time. It is thought that each year a country's productive capacity will usually increase because of advances in technology and improvements in education. It is estimated that the trend growth rate of the UK is 2.25 per cent per annum.

Sustained economic growth

For an economy to experience **sustained economic growth** (a continued increase in its output), it has to ensure that both its actual and its potential output continue to rise. If productive potential increases but demand does not rise to encourage producers to make use of the extra resources, output will not increase. There will be a *demand constraint*. Similarly if actual output matches potential output and potential output does not increase, there will be a *supply constraint* on future increases in output. Increases in aggregate demand will result only in inflation.

Figure 4(a) shows long-run aggregate supply (LRAS) increasing but output remaining unchanged because aggregate demand has not increased. Figure 4(b) shows aggregate demand increasing at the full capacity level which causes the price level to rise but output to remain unchanged.

Sustainable economic growth

What may limit economic growth in the longer run is the availability of natural resources and the earth's capacity to absorb waste. For example, intensive farming methods and large-scale fishing may increase some countries' output significantly in the short run. However in the long run, owing to the adverse effects on the fertility of land and the depletion of fishing stocks, these methods could result in lower output. Indeed, without care and appropriate policies there is the real risk that developed and developing countries may not be able to sustain economic growth. The quote at the beginning of the chapter may not prove to be correct.

In 1987, the World Commission on the Environment and Development produced the **Brundtland Report,** which was entitled *Our Common Future.* It defined sustainable development projects as those that meet the needs of the present generation in a way which

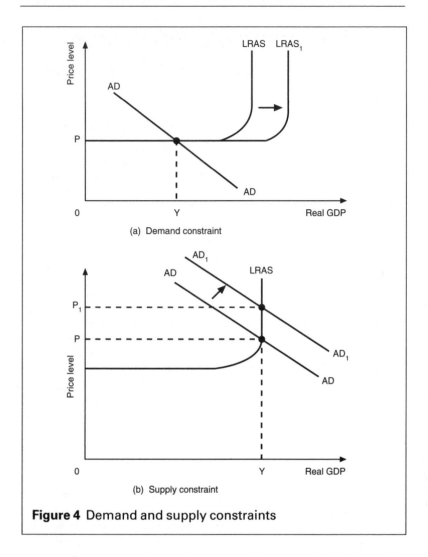

Figure 4 Demand and supply constraints

protects the environment for future generations, and looks after their expected needs as well. This report has helped to shape the World Bank's approach to development projects and has influenced United Nations conferences on the environment

So economists are increasingly urging that what countries should aim for is **sustainable economic growth** (see the accompanying extract from a *Guardian* article 'Green accounting: the real cost of living in Britain' by C. Denny and J. Vidal). This means a growth rate which can be continued over generations. To achieve this resources have to be used

Economic growth versus sustainable economic growth

CHARLOTTE DENNY and JOHN VIDAL

Consider the following. Since 1972, gross domestic product – the annual output of the economy has risen one-and-a-half times. During the same period, violent crime has quadrupled, the number of workless households has tripled and the incidence of asthma has tripled.

Steady economic growth, measured by rising GDP, is the holy grail for most policy-makers. But some economists wonder why. Despite the growth in GDP per head in most European countries since the early 70s, there is no evidence that people on the whole are much more content than they used to be.

Part of the problem is that GDP takes no account of the drawbacks of economic activity – pollution, congestion, and the loss of the natural environment. It is simply a measure of the output of goods and services in the economy over the year. Rising output equals rising incomes, but not necessarily higher living standards.

As well as failing to measure quality of life, many environmentalists say that GDP doesn't address whether current economic activity is sustainable.

Much economic activity – particularly in the industrial sector – exploits the earth's natural resources for its raw materials or uses the environment as a dustbin for unwanted by-products. Many of these resources are non-renewable and the environment's capacity to absorb pollution is limited.

Measuring growth while failing to take account of the bill we are writing for future generations is, according to the green lobby, like a company reporting an operating profit while neglecting to mention that it is running down its assets. In the short term, it might buoy up the company's share price, but in the long term it will go out of business.

The Guardian, 22 May 1998

carefully. For example, where possible renewable energy resources (e.g. solar energy) should be used, materials should be recycled and production methods which minimize pollution should be adopted. Built-in obsolescence should be avoided, with goods being produced to last, and the pace of change should be one that people can feel comfortable with.

KEY WORDS	
Economic growth	Output gap
Recession	Overheating
Nominal GDP	Trend growth
Real GDP	Sustained economic growth
Actual growth	Brundtland Report
Potential growth	Sustainable economic growth
Productive capacity	

Further reading
Maunder, P., Myers, D., Wall, N. and Miller, R., Chapter 26 in *Economics Explained*, 3rd edn, Collins Educational, 1995.

Sloman, J., Chapter 13 in *Economics*, 3rd edn., Prentice Hall, 1997.

Smith, D., Chapter 1 in *UK Current Economic Policy*, 2nd edn, Heinemann Educational, 1999.

'The Economist', Chapter 4 in *Guide to Economic Indicators*, 3rd edn, *The Economist*/Profile Books, 1997.

Useful websites
ONS: www.ons.gov.uk/
UN Statistics Division: www.un.org/depts/unsd/

Essay topics
1. (a) Distinguish between actual and potential growth. [10 marks]
   (b) Discuss the effects of a decrease in unemployment and an increase in the labour force on economic growth. [15 marks]
2. (a) Explain what is meant by sustainable economic growth. [10 marks]
   (b) Discuss why countries are becoming more concerned to ensure that their economic growth is sustainable. [15 marks]

Data response question
This task is based on a question set by the Oxford & Cambridge Schools Examination Board in 1997. Read the piece below, which is adapted from an article by David Smith in the *Sunday Times* in September 1996. Then answer the questions that follow.

The debate about growth

Kenneth Clarke [as Chancellor of the Exchequer] thinks that Britain's *trend growth rate* is nearer to 3 per cent than the Treasury's official 2.5 per cent estimate, itself revised up relatively recently from 2.25 per cent. This helps explain why he did not take issue with the Bank of England on the need for higher interest rates in 1994, when the economy grew by 4 per cent but has done since, when growth has been nearer to 2 per cent. The trend growth rate should be distinguished from growth prospects over the next two or three years. Thus, when the chancellor's advisors have suggested that Britain could grow at 3 per cent over the next three years without triggering inflation, they were not saying the trend growth rate had risen. Instead, their argument was that since growth had averaged only 2 per cent since the recovery began in 1992, there was scope for above-trend growth before *the output gap* was eliminated.

If the past is the best guide to the future, since 1979 Britain has averaged only 2 per cent growth a year, well below Clarke's 3 per cent. Although this period has included two recessions, and any final assessment should wait until we reach the peak of the current cycle, the record is not an impressive one. So what could be done to raise trend growth to 3 per cent? The simplest argument – stop central bankers with their anti-inflation obsession from holding back growth – is also the weakest. Martin Feldstein, the Harvard economist, argues that precisely the opposite is the case – in both the short and long term, low inflation is likely to be associated with stronger growth. In contrast, Patrick Minford believes that the UK has had a supply-side revolution, and that if the Bank only realized it we could have much faster growth, without any inflationary risk. More recently, Christopher Johnson has argued that *taking part in the European single currency could raise Britain's trend growth to 3 per cent.*

1. Why, in any given year, might the actual growth rate differ from the 'trend growth rate'? Why has the trend growth rate since 1979 been so low? [6 marks]
2. What is the significance of 'the output gap', and how might a professional economist attempt to estimate its size? [6 marks]
3. Outline the basis of the disagreement between Feldstein and Minford. [6 marks]
4. On what grounds might Johnson claim that 'taking part in the European single currency could raise Britain's trend growth to 3 per cent?' [7 marks]

Chapter Two

Causes of economic growth

'One of the most important questions in economics is: What causes economic growth and thus prosperity for the people of the world?'
R. Layard

Introduction

As the quote suggests, understanding the causes of economic growth is a crucial question which economists have analysed, and continue to do so.

In the short run, increases in output occur as a result of using existing resources more fully. As Figure 5 shows, an increase in aggregate demand (AD) causes a rise in output from OY to OY_1 as we move along the **long-run aggregate supply** (LRAS) line.

However, for output to continue to increase *in the long run* the productive capacity of the economy has to increase. Without an increase in the quantity and/or quality of resources, output cannot rise beyond the level corresponding to the full use of existing resources. There will be a **supply constraint**.

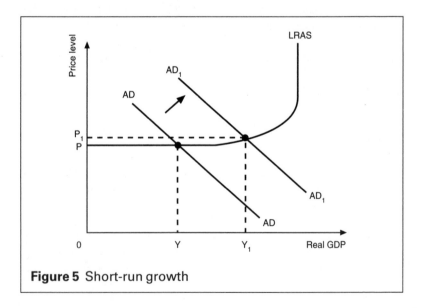

Figure 5 Short-run growth

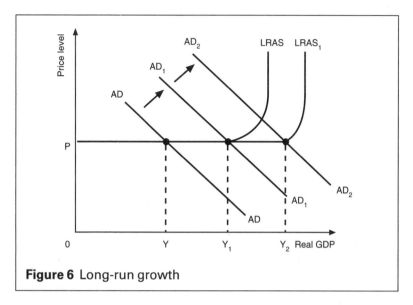

Figure 6 Long-run growth

Figure 6 illustrates an increase in the productive capacity of the economy by a shift of the LRAS curve to the right (to $LRAS_1$). This outward shift enables continuing increases in aggregate demand to be matched by higher output.

Short-run causes

If there is *spare capacity* in the economy, an increase in aggregate demand is likely to encourage producers to increase their output. The components of aggregate demand are:

● consumption
● investment
● government spending
● net exports – exports minus imports $(C + I + G + X - M)$.

However, producers will not raise output if they believe that the higher level of aggregate demand will not last. Fluctuating levels of aggregate demand may also make them reluctant to expand their output.

● Causes of an increase in aggregate demand

Aggregate demand will increase if any of its components rise, or if the rises in one or more of the components outweigh falls in the other components.

Table 2 shows the contributions that the changes in aggregate demand made to the UK's 3.5 per cent growth rate in 1997.

Table 2 Contributions to growth in constant-market-price GDP from 1996 to 1997

Component	Change in GDP	
	(£m)	(%)
Consumption	19 992	2.7
Government spending	37	0.0
Investment	8 680	0.2
Exports	18 371	2.5
Imports	−21 236	−2.9
Totals	25 844	3.5

Source: Adapted from ONS, National Income Accounts, Chart 1.3, *The Blue Book*, 1998

Consumption

Consumption is clearly the largest component of aggregate demand. It may increase for a number of reasons, especially the following:

- *A change in the buying population.* An increase in the population will obviously increase aggregate demand. There may be a natural increase in the population with the birth rate rising and/or the life expectancy rising. It could also result from net immigration. A change in the age structure of the population can also increase aggregate demand because the young tend to have a higher average propensity to consume (they spend a higher proportion of their income than the middle aged).
- *An increase in confidence in future prosperity.* When people are confident about their prospects they are likely to spend more now.
- *A fall in interest rates.* Lower interest rates discourage saving and encourage spending. The cost of borrowing falls and income is transferred from savers, whose discretionary income falls, to borrowers, whose discretionary income rises.
- *An increase in wealth.* If the value of the stock of assets people own rises, their ability and probably willingness to spend will increase.
- *A decrease in taxes.* A reduction in direct taxes increases disposable income, and again people's ability to spend. However, if it is the standard and higher rate or rates of income tax that are cut it will be the rich who benefit most. These are likely to have a low marginal propensity to consume.

- *An increase in transfer payments.* This may have a significant impact as recipients of state benefits have a high marginal propensity to consume.
- *An increase in the money supply.* More money in the economy will reduce the rate of interest and thereby increase consumption.

Investment
Investment is the most volatile component. Among the possible causes of an increase in investment are the following:

- *A fall in interest rates.* This raises the expected level of demand and reduces the cost of borrowing to spend on capital goods. It also lowers the opportunity cost of investment, since a reduced return on saving is given up when using retained profits to purchase capital goods.
- *A reduction in corporation tax.* This will increase both firms' ability and incentive to invest.
- *Improvements in technology.* Capital goods which embody more advanced technology have higher productivity.
- *Increased optimism.* Keynes referred to entrepreneurs' expectations as **'animal spirits'**. He argued that feelings of optimism (and pessimism) are very significant in influencing investment.

Government spending
Government spending may have to rise in several circumstances:

- *An ageing population.* This increases government spending on state pensions and healthcare.
- *A desire to raise educational standards.* This may increase government spending on education.
- *A perceived threat from a foreign power.* Defence spending is likely to rise in this situation.
- *Increasing crime.* A rise in crime or the fear of it is likely to cause increased spending on the police and legal system.
- *The implementation of policies designed to reflate the economy.* These policies may include reflationary fiscal policy (cutting taxes and/or raising government spending).

Net exports
Net exports (exports minus imports) may increase for a number of reasons:

- *Improvements in the design and quality of the country's goods and services.* This should increase demand for the country's goods and services at home and abroad.

- *Better marketing of the country's goods and services.* This will make people more aware of the good features of the goods and services.
- *Rises in productivity which lower costs.* The effect of this is to make the country's goods and services more price-competitive
- *A fall in the currency exchange rate.* A lower exchange rate reduces the price of a country's exports in terms of foreign currency and raises the price of imports in terms of the domestic currency.
- *A rise in incomes abroad.* Demand for many goods and services is income-elastic. When incomes abroad rise, foreigners demand more goods and services produced in their own and other countries. If the cause of the rise in aggregate demand and output is a rise in exports, this is referred to as **export-led growth.**

Long-run causes

As we have seen, for output to be able to continue to rise in the long run there must be an increase in the productive capacity of the economy. This can occur as a result of:

- an increase in the *quantity* of resources
  and/or
- an increase in the *quality* of resources.

● Increases in the quantity of resources

Resources include labour, capital and land.

Labour

The size of the labour force may rise as a result of a natural increase in the size of the population or by net immigration. Other causes include a reduction in the school leaving age, an increase in the retirement age, and an increase in the participation rate of mothers in the labour force. The last factor has been an important cause of the rise in the UK's labour force since the 1950s.

Capital

The stock of capital goods increases when **gross investment** (total investment) exceeds capital consumption (depreciation – i.e. capital goods bought to replace worn out ones). This positive difference is called **net investment.**

Whereas depreciation may leave potential output unchanged, or raise it if the replacement machines embody technological progress, *net investment must increase potential output.*

Net investment undertaken simply in order to keep pace with an increase in the supply of labour is known as **capital widening.** In contrast, increasing the amount of capital per worker is known as **capital deepening.**

By how much the new investment raises output depends on the productivity of the new capital. The **incremental capital output ratio** (ICOR) refers to the increase in output relative to net investment.

Firms will undertake new investment only if they believe that the yield from investment (which can be called the **marginal efficiency of capital,** or MEC) exceeds the cost.

A fall in the rate of interest for borrowing will reduce the cost of investment. If firms borrow to buy capital goods, there will be a reduction in the direct cost of investment, and if firms use retained profits to finance investment this will reduce the opportunity cost involved. More investment projects will now become profitable. Figure 7 shows a fall in the rest of interest causing a rise in planned investment.

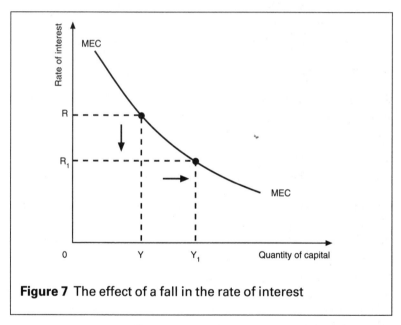

Figure 7 The effect of a fall in the rate of interest

More investment will be undertaken at any level of interest if the marginal efficiency of capital increases. There are a number of reasons why the expected rate of return on investment projects may rise. These include

- a reduction in corporation tax
- improvements in technology

- investment subsidies
- a reduction in the cost of capital goods
- increased confidence about future demand
- an increase in the growth of national income and hence demand for consumer goods.

The last influence is thought to be particularly significant and its importance is emphasized by the **accelerator theory**.

The accelerator theory

The accelerator theory states that the level of net investment depends on the rate of change of national income. Firms invest when the expected yield exceeds the cost of investment. If demand is increasing, firms will expect to sell more goods and hence receive a greater return. The theory also states that demand for capital goods fluctuates more than the demand for consumer goods.

For example, if one machine makes 100 goods and demand is initially 800 consumer goods, eight machines will be used. One machine may wear out each year and be replaced. If national income rises, demand will increase, for example, to 1000. This will be a rise in demand for consumer goods of 25 per cent. Now three fresh machines will be required, one as a replacement (depreciation) and two to expand capacity (net investment). So investment will rise by a greater percentage, 200 per cent.

However the accelerator theory does not provide a complete explanation of the behaviour of net investment. Demand for consumer goods may rise without a greater percentage rise in demand for capital goods. Indeed there may be no change in investment. Alternatively, firms may not invest to expand capacity if they do not believe that the increase in demand for consumer goods will last. **Expectations** are a significant influence on investment. If firms are pessimistic about the future they even may not replace some machines as they wear out.

Firms may also not buy new capital goods if they already have *spare capacity*. They will be able to respond to a rise in demand by making use of previously unused or under-used capital equipment and plant.

So spare capacity in the consumer goods industries may result in no change or a smaller change in demand for capital goods. In contrast it might be an absence of spare capacity in the capital goods industry which may prevent firms from being able to purchase more capital equipment.

Changes in technology may also mean that an increase in demand for consumer goods can bring about a smaller percentage increase in demand for capital goods. A new machine, embodying advanced technology, will be able to produce more capital goods than the machine, or machines, it replaces. Other influences on investment may change to offset the stimulus of rising demand.

Investment may also increase if there is an improvement in *entrepreneurial skills*. Entrepreneurs are more likely to take advantage of the profitable investment opportunities open to them and to be more willing to take calculated risks.

Figure 8 shows the marginal efficiency of capital (and hence planned investment) increasing.

The effect on output of an increase in investment will depend on what the investment relates to. In order to have a significant impact on output it should be in industries that are producing goods and services in high and growing world demand. Some economists are currently expressing concern that Europe's ageing population will mean that a relatively high proportion of investment resources will be devoted to projects with inherent low productivity (e.g. residential homes for care of the elderly or infirm).

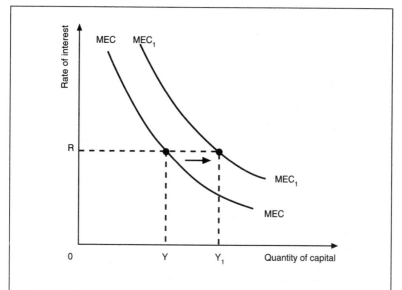

Figure 8 The effect of an increase in the marginal efficiency of capital

Land

Increases in natural resources result from land reclamation and discovery of new raw materials, such as oil and natural gas. However, in practice, land reclamation is not a significant factor, and the discovery of new raw materials is largely a matter of luck.

Even when new raw materials are discovered they usually provide only short-term growth. This is because once their rate of extraction is at a maximum, growth ceases. Output will remain at the new higher level until the raw materials start to wear out. When this occurs output will start to fall.

- ● Assessing the importance of increases in the quantity of resources

In most developed countries the main resource which increases over time is capital; labour tends to increase at a slower rate. In contrast, in some developing countries the supply of labour tends to increase at a faster rate than the supply of capital.

Increases in land tend to be more important in developing countries than in developed ones. However, in both types of economies land is relatively fixed. This leads to the possibility that *diminishing returns* may occur. So when all factors of production increase, the rate of growth is likely to slow down. It is not enough that labour and capital increase if there is a limited supply of land and raw materials. *The solution to this problem of diminishing returns is an increase in the productivity of resources.*

Causes of an increase in the quality of resources

An increase in the *quality* of resources means that they become more productive. Among the causes of an increase in quality are technological progress, investment in healthcare, and education and training.

- ● Technological progress

Some economists argue that the main determinant of long-run growth is the rate of **technological progress** combined with the development of institutions and attitudes which encourage the use of inventions (i.e. **innovation**).

Technological progress can refer to the development of new products, such as digital televisions and mobile telephones. This has two stages: one is product innovation, which is the introduction of a new product by a firm, and product diffusion, which is the introduction of similar new products by other firms.

However, it is technological progress in the form of *improvements in the methods of production and the quality of capital goods* which increases productivity and lowers costs.

Disembodied technological progress consists of advances in knowledge which do not require investment but rather a change in the way existing resources are used. This can increase productive capacity by freeing up resources to be used elsewhere in the economy. The production of capital goods which embody new technology will encourage firms to replace old capital with newer, more productive capital – such as more advanced computers and communication systems.

The rate of technological progress will depend on:

- the level and quality of research and development (R&D) in industry and higher education which influences the rate of invention
- the willingness and ability to accept change which influences the rate of innovation.

These are in turn influenced by education, training and the market structure in which firms operate.

● Healthcare

Investment in healthcare should result in a healthy labour force. Fewer days will be lost through illness and disease, and people will be fitter whilst at work. This should result in an increase in the quantity and quality of output.

● Education and training

Investment in **human capital** (i.e. spending on education and training) should raise educational standards and skill levels. The more educated and skilled the labour force is, the higher will be the productivity per worker. Increases in the quality and quantity of secondary school education are thought to have been one of the causes of the increase in the rate of growth of the so-called Asian tiger economies in the first half of the 1990s. However, as the item reproduced here from the *Guardian* discusses (page 22), education provision varies significantly throughout the world.

The quality of the education and training is important. Raising the level of provision will not have much impact if it is in areas that are not appropriate to the current and future needs of the economy.

Lesson the world must learn

LARRY ELLIOTT

The reasons governments in the west are looking to increase educational attainment is the recognition that human capital will be crucial to growth prospects in the next century. It is no longer endowments of physical capital that matter, but brain power. It is not just a question of importing technology from the west (although there are fewer telephone lines in sub-Saharan Africa than in Tokyo) but of integrating it into the economy. For that, a large pool of skilled labour is crucial.

The poorest countries in the world simply do not have this human structure. Only 7 per cent of sub-Saharan Africans receive a tertiary education, essentially because so few make it through the primary and secondary school system. The average five-year-old in sub-Saharan Africa can expect to receive four to six years of education; a child in the west 15–17 years.

Nor is it just a question of the quantity of education. Where the British government is dedicated to cutting class sizes for the five-to-seven age group to 30 or fewer, in parts of Africa and Asia it is not unusual to find 80 children per class. Teachers are often untrained and so poorly paid that they may be doing a second job to make ends meet.

Among the rich western countries that make up the Organisation for Economic Co-operation and Development, an average of $4636 is spent per pupil on primary and secondary education. In the developing world it is $165.

Although Britain spends less than the OECD average, at $3553, that is still 130 times more than in Zambia.

The lesson of South Korea shows what can be done. There, heavy and sustained investment in education from the early 1960s onward predated the rapid increase in growth and living standards in the 1970s and 1980s. South Korea in effect short-circuited the development process by providing itself with western levels of education, but the chance of something similar occurring in sub-Sarahan Africa are remote.

The Guardian, 22 March 1999

KEY WORDS

Long-run aggregate supply	Incremental capital output ratio
Supply constraint	Marginal efficiency of capital
Animal spirits	Accelerator theory
Export-led growth	Expectations
Gross investment	Technological progress
Net investment	Innovation
Capital widening	Human capital
Capital deepening	

Further reading

Beardshaw, J. *et al.*, Chapter 4 in *Economics: A Student's Guide*, 4th edn, Addison-Wesley Longman, 1998.

Buxton, T., Chapman, P. and Temple, P., Chapter 4 in *Britain's Economic Performance*, 2nd edn, Routledge, 1998.

Grant, S., Chapter 55 in *Stanlake's Introductory Economics*, 7th edn, Addison-Wesley Longman, 1999.

Smith, D., Chapter 6 in *UK Current Economic Policy*, 2nd edn, Heinemann Educational, 1999.

Useful websites

OECD: www.oecd.org/std/index.htm
The Guardian: www.guardian.co.uk/

Essay topics

1. (a) Distinguish between short-run and long-run causes of economic growth. [10 marks]
   (b) Assess the importance of education as a cause of economic growth. [15 marks]
2. Using the aggregate demand and supply model, analyse the effects of an increase in investment on the general price level. [22 marks]
   [University of Oxford Delegacy of Local Examinations 1997]

Data response question

This task is based on a question set by the Associated Examining Board in 1998. Study the piece below and the data in the five charts (all adapted from *Lloyds Bank Economic Bulletin*, September 1995) and then answer the questions that follow.

The investment puzzle

The current recovery [i.e. in 1995] is an unusual one in many respects. It owes more to a strong export performance, and much less to a surge in consumer spending, than is normal. Furthermore, fixed capital investment has made little contribution to this recovery, which is worrying for the longer term sustainability of the upturn.

We are now three years into a recovery which began in the second quarter of 1992. However, aggregate investment levels remain nearly 5 per cent *below* the level of investment in the first quarter of 1992. In part the failure of aggregate business investment to recover is due to the relatively high levels of investment in the recession by the utilities sector and by the oil and gas sector. Both of these were *non-cyclical* phenomena, the former being due to a post-privatization upsurge, the latter being due to new fields being developed in the North Sea.

Figure A shows business investment as a percentage of gross domestic product (GDP) since the depth of the previous recession in 1981, while Figure B provides an indication of spare capacity in manufacturing industry.

Figure A Business investment as a percentage of GDP

Figure B Percentage of manufacturing firms working below capacity

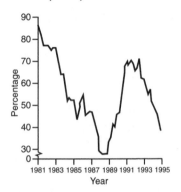

Figure C shows the profits of companies, measured as a percentage of capital employed, while Figure D shows the cost of capital reflected in the

Figure C Percentage net rates of return for industrial and commercial companies

Figure D Cost of capital (percentage interest) for manufacturing industry

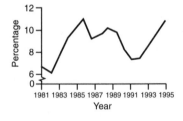

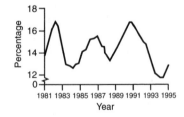

Figure E Factors likely to limit capital investment

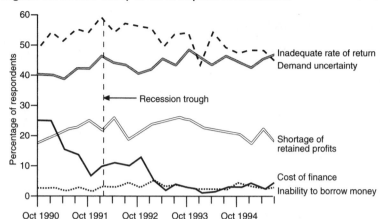

rate of interest firms have to pay to borrow money for investment. Finally, Figure E shows the factors which members of the Confederation of British Industry (CBI) said acted as a constraint on their investment spending.

1. (a) Why do economists consider that the level of aggregate investment expenditure is likely to be influenced by the extent of spare capacity available to companies? [3 marks]
   (b) To what extent do the data in Figures A and B support the view that there is a relationship between the extent of spare capacity in manufacturing industry and investment expenditure? [4 marks]
2. Using the data to illustrate your answer, discuss other factors which are likely to influence the level of aggregate investment expenditure in the UK. [10 marks]
3. Assess the importance of aggregate investment for the future prospects of the UK economy. [13 marks]

Chapter Three

Growth theories

'If countries understood better the path to higher growth they would take it. Explaining growth is, alas, one of those many problems to which economists have only the most partial of answers.'
Hamish McRae

As mentioned in the previous chapter, economists seek to explain the causes of economic growth. However, as the opening quote suggests, it is neither a straightforward nor an easy task.

The nature of growth theories

Most, but not all, growth theories focus on the *supply factors* which influence the development of productive capacity.

What growth theories seek to do is to identify the key determinant or determinants of economic growth. By doing this they seek to explain why growth rates differ between countries.

As well as drawing on economic theory, economists make use of empirical work. Considerable statistical analysis has been undertaken checking the correlation between economic growth rates and, for example, inflation, investment, government spending, years of education and even fertility rates.

However, whilst it may be found, for example, that countries that have high levels of investment also have high growth rates, it can be difficult to determine whether it is the high investment that causes economic growth or whether it is economic growth that leads to high levels of investment. In practice it may be a mixture of both – a **virtuous circle**.

Key determinants of growth

Among the influences which economists identify as playing a crucial role in economic growth are:

- investment
- the stage of economic development
- export performance
- inflation
- stability
- the size of the public sector
- investment in human capital.

● Investment

A number of economists emphasize the role of investment. They argue that high growth rates in economies have nearly always been associated with high levels of investment.

By devoting a significant proportion of resources to investment, countries can build up capital stock which can be used to produce higher output in future years.

Capital accumulation is particularly important for economies where labour input is not increasing significantly. As noted in Chapter 2, if capital deepening occurs not only may production increase but so will productivity.

Investment is seen as being particularly important as it increases both aggregate demand and aggregate supply. Investment is one of the components of aggregate demand, and an increase in investment will cause GDP to rise by a multiple amount. Investment is an **injection** into the **circular flow of income**. The extra expenditure on capital goods will generate a rise in income which will in turn be spent. Income will rise until injections again equal **leakages**. If, for example, the multiplier is three, an increase in investment of £10 billion will cause GDP (output) to rise by £30 billion.

As well as increasing aggregate demand, investment will increase the productive potential of the country. So investment creates the resources to produce the extra demand created.

Figure 9 (on page 28) compares the Keynesian and new classical versions of the effects of an increase in investment. Output will increase but the effect on the price level will depend on the relative sizes of the shifts in the AD and LRAS curves.

As countries accumulate more capital there is the risk that *diminishing returns* may set in. Some economists claim that this explains why some countries with large stocks of capital goods receive lower rates of return on new capital. However, as well as the quantity of capital the quality of capital is also important. For example, investment in infrastructure, which includes roads, schools and hospitals, may have a smaller, more long-run effect on economic growth than investment in high-tech industries.

Empirical studies do suggest that high investment is associated with rapid economic growth. However, most of these studies indicate that investment is not enough by itself and, as already mentioned, the causality may run in the opposite direction. Higher economic growth will generate the savings needed for investment.

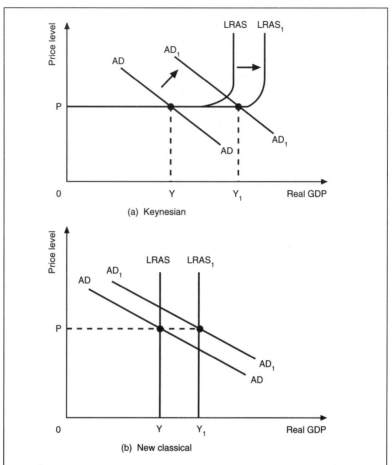

Figure 9 The effects of an increase in investment according to the Keynesian and new classical schools

● The stage of economic development

Nicholas Kaldor, the Cambridge economist, argued in the 1960s that the rate of economic growth depends on the **stage of economic development** a country has reached. He believed that economic growth is fastest when countries approach maturity. At this stage workers move from the primary into the secondary sector. He argued that a large manufacturing sector is the major driving force behind economic growth as it is in this sector where economies of scale are most significant.

He explained that the UK economy experiences relatively slow growth as a result of having a small manufacturing sector, with most of the population being employed in the tertiary sector. His supporters point out that rapid economic growth in Vietnam has been associated with a transfer of labour from agriculture to manufacturing.

However, critics of Kaldor's view argue that productivity growth is higher in rapidly growing economies than in slowly growing economies *in all sectors*, not just in manufacturing.

• Export performance
In countries that are heavily dependent on international trade, such as the UK, there seems to be a close association between rapid rates of increase in exports and high growth rates. Rapid increases in exports appear to depend primarily on price competitiveness which, in turn, is closely connected with changes in wage costs per unit.

There are thought to be various ways in which the growth of exports affects overall economic growth.

Entrepreneurial confidence
If exports rise rapidly, entrepreneurs will be less worried that the government will restrict increases in aggregate demand for fear of a current account deficit arising. This will make them more willing to invest and expand output. In the absence of a good export performance there will be a balance of payments constraint. In the long run the economy cannot grow faster than at the rate which will sustain a balance of payments equilibrium. As an economy grows more imports will be purchased and it is important that exports can rise proportionately to pay for them. So a country with a good export performance will be able to sustain a higher rate of economic growth.

Wider markets
A healthy export market will mean that entrepreneurs will be less dependent on the home market where aggregate demand could be falling or fluctuating.

Competitiveness
Competitive export markets increase the size of firms' markets, encouraging them to increase investment and enabling them to take greater advantage of economies of scale. Both of these linked effects should raise productivity and thus make firms more price-competitive.

• Inflation
Some economists state that high growth is associated with low and

stable inflation. They argue that low and stable inflation can encourage economic growth in a number of ways:

- entrepreneurs will not be worried that the government will adopt deflationary policies
- planning is easier and less costly
- menu, shoe leather and administrative costs are low
- low levels of nominal interest rates may encourage borrowing.

A high and unstable inflation rate discourages economic growth because of the uncertainty it creates and the costs it imposes on consumers and producers. A negative inflation rate (i.e. the price level falling) would also discourage economic growth. Falling prices reduce confidence and cause consumers to delay their purchases. The resulting fall in demand causes firms to cut back on output.

- Stability

It is not just instability in terms of the price level which can discourage economic growth. Frequent and unpredictable changes in, for example, interest rates and taxes makes it difficult for consumers and producers to plan ahead. Table 3 shows stability rankings produced by Lloyds Bank.

Table 3 Stability rankings, 1980–96

Overall	Output	Inflation	Interest rates	Government finance*
Austria	Austria	Germany	Japan	USA
Netherlands	France	Austria	Netherlands	Netherlands
Germany	Switzerland	Japan	Germany	Austria
Japan	Netherlands	Switzerland	Austria	France
Switzerland	Belgium	Netherlands	Switzerland	Australia
USA	Italy	Belgium	USA	Germany
France	Japan	USA	Sweden	Italy
Belgium	USA	Canada	Canada	Spain
Canada	Germany	Australia	France	Canada
Australia	Australia	Sweden	Spain	Japan
Sweden	Sweden	Spain	Belgium	UK
Italy	Canada	UK	UK	Belgium
Spain	Spain	France	Australia	Sweden
UK	UK	Italy	Italy	

* Excluding Switzerland, for which no comparable data are available.
Source: *Lloyds Bank Economic Bulletin*, no. 13, February 1997.

Figure 10 shows, according to *Lloyds Bank Economic Bulletin*, 'some evidence of a negative relationship between instability and economic growth [for the 14 countries in Table 3]. A strong relationship should not be expected, because instability affects growth only with a lag.'

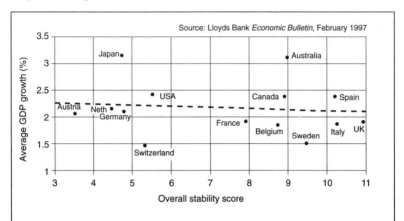

Figure 10 Relationship between stability scores and growth: the broken line shows an attempt at a 'best fit'

● Size of the government sector

Economists disagree about the amount of government intervention that is beneficial for economic growth. New Classical economists, who believe that markets work efficiently, support low government spending and minimal intervention to encourage, for example, competition and promotion.

In contrast, Keynesian economists, who think that market failure is a major problem, favour a higher level of government intervention. They believe that economies are inherently unstable if left to market forces, with output levels fluctuating and with no guarantee that they will operate at the full-employment level. They support government intervention, for example in the form of investment subsidies, to promote economic growth.

● Investment in human capital

Empirical work suggests that countries that have high levels of education and training relative to their physical capital are likely to grow at a faster rate than those with less. Supporters of this view point to the high rates of economic growth experienced by the likes of

Singapore, China and India in the early 1990s when they were significantly increasing spending on secondary education.

Theories of economic growth

The first six theories examined here concentrate on how developing economies can grow. The last three theories (new classical, endogenous and convergence) are concerned with investigating the forces which inter-react to cause economic growth, and with explaining why countries grow at different rates.

● The Harrod–Domar model

This was developed in the 1930s by the British economist Roy **Harrod** and the American economist Evsey **Domar**. It was not initially intended to explain economic development but it has been widely used by economic planners working in and with developing countries.

It argues that the savings ratio, investment and technological change are the key variables in determining economic growth. The theory can be expressed by the equation

$$g \text{ (economic growth)} = s/k,$$

where s is the savings ratio and k is the ratio of capital to output. The greater the level of savings, then, the greater the level of investment and so the faster the rate of economic growth, especially if the investment embodies improved technology.

The model implies that if economic planners know the savings ratio and the capital/output ratio they can calculate the rate of economic growth. It also suggests that a target rate can be set for economic growth, and that then the savings ratio required to obtain it can be calculated. In addition it can be used to set employment targets if it is assumed that there is a predictable relationship between output and economic growth.

However, the model has been criticized on a number of grounds. One is its assumptions of a closed (self-contained) economy and a fixed capital/output ratio. Another is that it may not be the level of savings which restricts investment but the lack of profitable investment opportunities.

● Rostow's stages of economic growth

Walt **Rostow**, an American economist, studied the historical record of industrialized countries and made use of the Harrod–Domar model in developing his own theory, again emphasizing the importance of savings and investment. He argued that all countries follow the same stages of economic development but are at different stages. He identified five stages:

Traditional
In the traditional society, *barter* occurs and agriculture is the most important industry.

Transitional
In the transitional stage the preconditions for *take-off* occur, including a rise in the savings ratio, development of foreign trade and the emergence of entrepreneurs.

Take-off
This is the key stage at which growth becomes self-sustaining and there is a *virtuous circle of economic development.*

Rostow argued that there are certain conditions necessary for a country to take off towards economic prosperity. These include a rise in the rate of saving and investment ratios above 10 per cent, the development of a strong manufacturing sector, and the existence of a political, social and institutional framework which fosters economic growth.

This stage got its name from the analogy with an aircraft which can fly only after achieving a critical speed.

Drive to maturity
At this stage the economy has moved away from being a developing economy and is moving towards the status of a developed economy.

Age of mass consumption
This occurs when the economy has reached the developed level and its people are able to enjoy high living standards.

Rostow argued that countries could reach the take-off stage by following a set of rules, in particular raising investment via increased savings. He stated that the UK reached the take-off stage in the 1780s, the USA in the 1820s and Japan in 1910, and that some countries were still in the first two stages.

This model has not escaped criticism. It has been argued in particular that, while high levels of savings and investment are indeed important conditions for economic growth, they are not *sufficient* conditions. For example, people may choose to invest their savings in another country, and not all investment is productive. Economic growth is also influenced by other factors, including infrastructure and education.

Not many economists now believe that there are definite stages of economic growth with distinctive savings and capital/output ratios.

Nor do they think that development finishes with the last stage. It is now thought that whilst there are common features in economic development, each country's path is unique.

● The Lewis model

W. Arthur **Lewis**, a West Indian economist, published a paper in 1954 entitled 'Economic development with unlimited supplies of labour'. This put forward a structural-change model and focused on the means by which an economy is changed from one relying on agriculture to one in which the manufacturing and tertiary sectors dominate.

He argued that economies that had unlimited supplies of relatively cheap labour could grow rapidly by transferring workers from low-productivity agriculture to high-productivity manufacturing and tertiary industries. He described a *dual economy*:

- one sector was a largely rural, traditional and non-capitalist one in which workers were self-employed in family units
- the other (smaller) sector was an urban, capitalist and industrialized one in which labour was hired and firms sold their output for a profit.

The latter sector, which had a higher wage rate, could obtain labour initially without having to raise its wage rate from the former economy in which there would be unemployed or under-employed labour. The effect on agricultural output would be minimal as the workers' marginal productivity was zero. Unemployment and under-employment would gradually decline as the workers were absorbed into the capitalist sector. Once this occurred the economy would be transformed into a modern, urban and industrialized country.

The Lewis model was interpreted as favouring an import-substitution and industrialization growth strategy for developing countries. It is now thought that for some developing countries small-scale rural investment might provide a more appropriate route to development.

The Lewis model, too, has come in for criticism on a number of grounds.

- What appear to be under-employed workers may actually be migrant workers who undertake key functions in the agricultural community at peak times and already work in industry in off-peak times.
- Whilst there might be a large supply of unskilled labour, there may still be a shortage of skilled workers and a shortage of entrepreneurs to expand the capitalist sector.

- Workers may also not move to the capitalist sector if there is insufficient demand for the goods and services being produced in that sector.
- Empirical evidence shows that in many developing countries there is still unemployment and under-employment in both the agricultural and industrialized sectors.

The balanced-growth theory

The **balanced-growth** theory argues that to achieve development there should be a carefully managed process of economic growth, with industries developing steadily and growing at the same rate – thereby creating markets for each other and the opportunity to benefit from the external economies of scale each one creates.

The example often used to support this view is that growth in the shoe industry should be accompanied by growth in, for example, the publishing and brewing industries, if what people want is a greater quantity and quality of shoes, books and beer.

This theory was supported by the empirical work of Simon Kuznets, a Russian economist, who studied the experience of thirteen countries.

The balanced-growth theory is sometimes known as the 'big-push theory of industrialization'. It suggests the need for state intervention to coordinate the process and overcome supply and demand imbalances by, for example, training workers and ensuring the availability of investment finance.

The unbalanced-growth theory

The **unbalanced-growth** theory, attributed to an American economist, Albert Hirschman, argues that economic growth is usually unbalanced and that planners should recognize this.

Hirschman suggested that planners should seek to promote the expansion of key industries which can benefit other industries via **backward and forward linkages**. A backward linkage connects the industry to the suppliers of its raw materials and inputs, whereas a forward linkage connects it with the industries that purchase its output.

The backwardness hypothesis

The **backwardness hypothesis** was developed principally by the Russian economist Alexander Gerschenkron. He argued that countries can take advantage of being initially less developed by copying the more advanced technology and skills of developed countries and by attracting capital investment from them. He thought this would enable them to jump some of the stages of economic growth and grow more rapidly than developed countries. Indeed the more 'backward' a country was the greater its potential for rapid growth. This was a forerunner of the convergence theories discussed below.

● The new classical (or neoclassical) theory

The **new classical theory** is rather pessimistic about the prospects for economic growth. It suggests that as the stock of capital increases, diminishing returns set in, causing economic growth to slow and eventually cease. In order to offset this tendency and keep growing the economy must benefit from continual injections of technological progress.

According to this model, poorer countries will grow more rapidly than richer ones. This is because poorer countries will start with less capital and so should gain higher returns from each unit of investment. The model seeks to explain the success of the so-called Asian tigers in the 1980s and first half of the 1990s by their rapid accumulation of capital and labour.

However, despite some exceptions, most rich countries have faster rates of economic growth than poor ones.

● New growth (or endogenous growth) theory

New growth theory explicitly includes technological progress and provides a more optimistic view of the prospects for economic growth.

The model suggests that diminishing returns do not need to apply because of the improvements in education, training and technological progress which economic growth itself generates. A growing economy can afford to devote more resources to education, training and R&D. Firms will be stimulated to innovate by the desire to gain a competitive advantage and earn higher profits.

Improvements in education and training and technological progress increase productivity. They also have positive *externalities*. This is because they stimulate improvements in other firms and countries which can copy new methods and products, hire better-trained and educated workers, and take advantage of higher-quality equipment, components and services (see the article from *The Economist*).

● Convergence theory

While the new classical theory argues that the growth rates of poor economies will be higher than those of rich ones because of diminishing returns, more modern **convergence models** take a wider perspective. For example, Charles Feinstein, Professor of Economic History at Oxford University, has argued that the levels of output of countries will move towards each other as he believes that there is an inverse

The chemistry of growth

The dominant family of theories is still organized around the 'neoclassical' model of growth first devised by Robert Solow of MIT more than 40 years ago. These theories have the property that a sustained increase in investment increases the economy's growth rate only temporarily: the ratio of capital to labour goes up, the marginal product of capital declines and the economy moves back to a long-term path, with output growing at the same rate as the workforce (quality-adjusted, in more recent versions) plus a factor to reflect improving 'productivity'. Because this last term is exogenous, meaning determined outside the model, critics say that the neoclassical theory of growth ignores the very engine of growth.

The other main approach, which has also spawned an extended family of models, goes by the name of 'endogenous growth' theory. The idea was to bring improvements in productivity, notably due to innovation, and to investments in human capital, fully inside the model – so that ongoing economic growth emerged as a natural consequence. One line of attack is based on the idea of 'externalities' in investment; another concerns itself with the variety of additions to capital (as opposed to mere increases in quantity); yet another tries to take seriously Schumpeter's ideas (hitherto neglected in mainstream economic thought) on obsolescence and 'creative destruction'. Some of these departures have now been 'promising' for a suspiciously long time.

The Economist, 6 March 1999

relationship between levels of output and rates of economic growth.

The view is that rich countries will grow less rapidly than less rich countries. This means that the initially less rich countries catch up with the rich ones. They also go on to overtake them. Once this occurs, however, their growth rates slow down whilst the growth rates of the countries they have overtaken start to rise.

It is argued that rich countries tend to grow slowly because:

- they rely on working practices, customs, education and institutions which initially made them successful but which have become out of date
- they see technological progress and innovation as a threat to established methods and products
- they are initially at the forefront of research and development and have no one to copy from
- their populations will want to relax and enjoy the benefits of high output in the forms of increased leisure and consumption.

In contrast, less rich countries will grow more rapidly because:

- their populations will not be satisfied with their living standards and will be prepared to work hard to catch up
- they will recognize the need to change attitudes and institutions to promote economic growth
- technological progress will be welcomed
- they can learn from leading countries – being able to copy and adapt R&D, technology and best examples of management systems, industrial relations and financial markets
- they may have workers who can be reallocated into more productive sectors of the economy.

KEY WORDS

Virtuous circle	Lewis model
Capital accumulation	Balanced growth
Injection	Unbalanced growth
Circular flow of income	Backward and forward linkages
Leakages	Backwardness hypothesis
Stage of economic development	New classical theory
Harrod–Domar model	New growth theory
Rostow model	Convergence models

Further reading

Anderton, A., Unit 99 in *Economics*, 2nd edn., Causeway Press, 1995.

Barro, R., Chapter 1 in *Determinants of Economic Growth*, MIT Press, 1997.

Mankiw, N., Chapter 24 in *Principles of Economics*, Dryden Press, 1998.

Sloman, J., Chapter 13 in *Economics*, 3rd edn, Prentice Hall, 1997.

Useful websites

Lloyds Bank *Economic Reports*: www.lloydsbank-corporate.co.uk/
The Economist: www.economist.com/

Essay topics

1. (a) Explain the meaning of 'economic growth' and discuss how it can be measured. [10 marks]
   (b) Over the period 1989–94 the Italian economy grew by only 5.2 per cent, whereas there was 11.2 per cent growth in Germany. Discuss why growth rates might differ between countries. [15 marks] [OCR Modular, National Economy paper, 1998]

2. Use the concepts of aggregate demand and supply to analyse the effects of an increase in fixed capital on national income, consumption, imports and prices. [25 marks] [University of Oxford Delegacy of Local Examinations, specimen paper, 1996]

Data response question

This task is based on a question set by the University of Oxford Delegacy of Local Examinations in 1997. Read the piece below and study the table. In answering the questions that follow you should use not only the information given, but also your own knowledge of economics, economic analysis and economic institutions.

Changes in the nature of investment

One of the recent puzzles in economics relates to investment. It simply doesn't behave as it used to. For example, even though interest rates have been falling, investment expenditure seems to have remained fairly stable.

One possible explanation is that, because of the recent rapid technical advances in computers and electronics, the price of many investment goods has fallen sharply in real terms, and their productivity has increased. So now you can replace your plant more cheaply than before, and get increased productivity and capacity as well.

Several things flow from this. To start with, there is an implication that one of the important barriers to entry has been reduced, with consequential effects on market structures and the nature of competition. Secondly, there must be a shift away from labour towards capital, with implications for employment and unemployment, differential effects on wages and earnings by skill, possible differences between the sexes, and between regions.

Again, if investment is now relatively cheap and less responsive to interest rate changes, the government may have to rethink macroeconomic policy. The investment multiplier may not have changed, but the ability to boost investment has. The government may have to place more reliance on other forms of expenditure to kickstart the economy.

Table A Investment in the UK, 1986–95

Year	Gross fixed capital formation (£bn at 1990 prices)	Profits (£bn at 1990 prices)	Average earnings index (1990 = 100)	Gross national product (£bn at 1990 prices)	Employment index (1990 = 100)
1986	83.7	71.1	71.3	493.3	91.0
1987	92.3	84.5	76.8	515.9	93.1
1988	105.2	86.6	83.5	543.2	96.2
1989	114.5	83.7	91.2	552.6	99.1
1990	107.6	75.5	100.0	551.8	100.0
1991	97.4	64.7	108.0	539.7	96.7
1992	96.0	64.5	114.6	541.1	94.7
1993	96.5	76.2	118.5	551.3	93.4
1994	99.5	91.4	123.3	580.2	93.8
1995	100.7	97.5	127.4	591.8	94.7

Source: *Economic Trends and Financial Statistics*, CSO.

1. (a) The article states that even though interest rates have been falling, investment expenditure seems to have remained fairly stable. Is this the relationship economic theory would predict? [4 marks]

   (b) Using the data in Table A, assess the relative importance of other factors which influence investment. [12 marks]

2. (a) Use economic analysis to show how changes in the nature of investment could affect earnings and the size of employment referred to in the third paragraph. [12 marks]

   (b) To what extent is there evidence in the table to support your argument in (a)? [8 marks]

3. (a) Explain carefully how the changes in the nature of investment could give rise to the changes in market structure suggested at the beginning of the third paragraph. [8 marks]

   (b) Evaluate the potential effect of these changes for consumers. [14 marks]

4. Assess the extent and nature of any changes in government policy to stimulate the economy that may have to be considered, given the change in the nature of investment. [22 marks]

Chapter Four

Comparative economic growth

'One of the basic economic facts which has increasingly entered into national consciousness is the relatively slow rate of economic growth of Britain.'
Nicholas Kaldor

Comparing economic growth rates

Economists and politicians compare economic growth rates over time and between countries. Stable economic growth, along with inflation, unemployment and the balance of payments position, is an indicator of a country's economic performance.

As mentioned in earlier chapters, an unstable growth rate will impose costs on a country. A growth rate which is below that of recent years and/or below that of other countries will also be likely to cause concern. This is because it implies that living standards are not rising very rapidly, that a gap may be opening up between the living standards in the country and those in other countries, and that output is rising below the trend level. In this case a government may consider it necessary to implement policies to stimulate economic activity.

Measurement problems

To make valid comparisons of economic growth, care has to be taken in measuring changes in output. In practice a number of problems arise in gaining an accurate measure. These occur mainly because some goods and services are not sold through the market and hence do not have a price attached to them.

To measure the output of government services for which a price is not charged – for example the police service and the NHS (National Health Service) – traditionally the government has used the cost of providing the services. This can give a misleading idea of what is happening to output since the greater the cost, the greater appears to be the output. If, say, the productivity of public sector employees increases it may be possible to increase the quantity and quality of public sector services at a lower cost. However, the official GDP figures would show a decrease in output. To overcome this problem, the Office for National Statistics (ONS), which produces statistical data for the

---

New method of measuring government output

Measuring the output of government at constant prices is problematic, as it is difficult to separate it into price and volume components. Currently for the UK, inputs rather than outputs are measured at constant prices, a process which does not take account of productivity changes.

The ONS has developed an improved methodology for measuring government output at constant prices. This measures outputs not inputs, and thus takes account of productivity changes. The new methodology covers education, health and social security (around 50 per cent of the public sector) using a range of performance indicators, such as pupil and student numbers for education; a cost-weighted activity index for hospital output; and numbers of benefit claims for social security.

Source: ONS, *The Blue Book*, 1998

---

government and other users, is developing a new way of measuring government output – see the boxed item.

There is also the problem of undeclared economic activity. This is referred to as the **black economy**; it includes the output of goods and services that are not declared because either the activities are illegal (e.g. the sale of hard drugs) or because those providing them wish to avoid paying tax. Governments usually make an estimate of the size of the black economy by examining the difference between GDP as measured by the expenditure method and GDP as measured by the income method. It has been estimated that whilst the size of the US black economy is equivalent to 9 per cent of its GDP and the UK's is equal to 12 per cent, the size of the black economy in Russia is the equivalent of an amazing and worrying 100 per cent.

Other services are not marketed because they are produced not for sale but for consumption by those producing them. These include DIY, cleaning and looking after children.

Interpretation problems over time
Higher growth rates suggest that economic performance has improved and that living standards are rising. However, as well as taking care in measuring changes in output, care has also to be taken in interpreting the findings.

- Changes in real GDP per head should be compared. This is because inflation would cause nominal (money) GDP to rise even if the output of goods and services had not changed. Similarly if increases

---

What is included in GDP?

Basically the decision whether to include a particular activity within the production boundary takes into account the following:

- Is the product of the activity marketable and does it have a market value?
- If the product does not have a meaningful market value, can a meaningful market value be assigned (i.e. can we impute a value)?
- Would exclusion (or inclusion) of the product of the activity make comparisons between countries or over time more meaningful?

In practice under ESA95 (the standard EU measure) the production boundary can be summarized as follows:

- the production of all goods, whether supplied to other units or retained by the producer for own final consumption or gross capital formation, and
- services only in so far as they have exchanged in the market and/or generate income for other economic units.

For households this has the result of including the production of goods on own-account, for example the produce of farms consumed by the farmer's own household. (However, in practice produce from gardens or allotments has proved impossible to estimate in the United Kingdom so far.) The boundary excludes the production of services for own final consumption (household domestic and personal services like cleaning, cooking, ironing and the care of children and the sick or infirm). Although the production of these services does take a considerable time and effort, the activities are self-contained with limited repercussions for the rest of the economy and, as the vast majority of household domestic and personal services are not produced for the market, it is very difficult to value the services in a meaningful way.

Source: ONS, *The Blue Book*, 1998

---

in GDP are matched by increases in population, living standards per head would not have increased.

- A country's growth rate may increase but it may be at the expense of higher levels of pollution and depletion of natural resources.
- More goods and services may be produced, but people will enjoy them less if their quality has fallen.
- The growth rate may rise, but if the distribution of income has become less evenly distributed only a relatively small number may benefit.

- A lower growth rate associated with shorter working hours and better working conditions may result in a greater improvement in living standards than a faster rate associated with longer working hours and a deterioration in working conditions.

- A rise in the growth rate may be the result of an increase in the output of what can be referred to as **regrettables**. These are goods and services which merely maintain rather than increase living standards. For example, increases in the provision of anti-pollution services, defence and the police service may occur to keep pace with higher pollution levels, increased threat from foreign powers and increased crime levels. The output of a range of goods and services (e.g. transport and financial services) may not be enjoyed for their own sake but are necessary for people to participate in the economy.

Interpretation problems involved in international comparisons

In comparing growth rates between countries it is also important to ensure that increases in real GDP per head are being examined. As with comparing changes in GDP over time, consideration should be taken of, for example, changes in the quality of goods being produced, working conditions, levels of pollution and the size of the black economy.

There are also differences in the proportion of economic activities which countries record. Countries also vary in terms of tastes, needs and the proportion of goods and services which are provided by the state.

In addition, where countries do not operate a single currency, GDP figures have to be changed into a common standard. If they are converted into, say, US dollars by using exchange rates, a misleading impression may be gained. This is because exchange rates may not reflect **purchasing power parities** and may, if the exchange rates are floating, change on a frequent basis. As a result comparisons are often made using not the official exchange rate but purchasing power parities (PPPs); that is, how much of the domestic currencies are needed to purchase a given basket of goods and services. For instance, if in the USA the basket would cost $60 whereas in the UK it would cost £30, the UK's GDP figures would be converted into dollars on the basis of $2 = £1.

Figure 11 shows a map which compares the GDP per head of the EU member countries (and regions) based on a purchasing power standard.

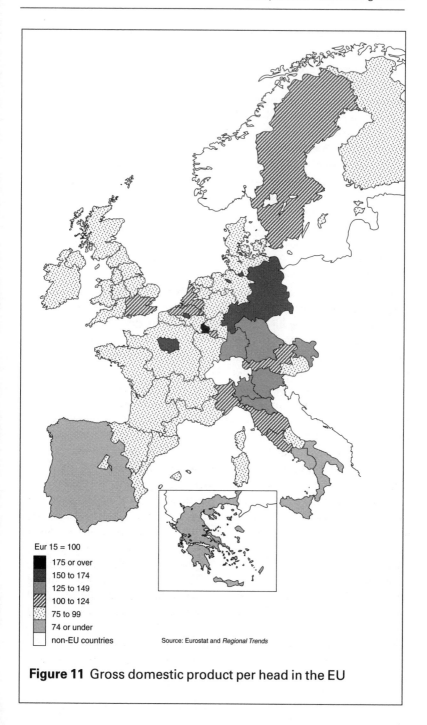

Eur 15 = 100

- ■ 175 or over
- 150 to 174
- 125 to 149
- 100 to 124
- 75 to 99
- 74 or under
- non-EU countries

Source: Eurostat and *Regional Trends*

Figure 11 Gross domestic product per head in the EU

Owing to the problems involved in using GDP figures to assess a country's economic performance and the living standards of its inhabitants, a number of suggestions have been made. These include assessing other data in addition to GDP and constructing alternative measures, particularly of welfare. One such alternative measure is the **human development index** (HDI). This takes into account not only GDP but also the amount of education and length of life the country's population can enjoy.

In November 1998 the UK government announced that it will publish thirteen **headline indicators of the quality of life** in the UK. These indicators include not only changes in real GDP but also environmental indicators, such as greenhouse gas emissions and quantity of waste, and social welfare indicators such as average life expectancy and educational qualifications.

The UK's economic growth

As the quote at the beginning of the chapter indicates, concern has been expressed about the relatively slow growth rate of the UK. Economists and politicians have also been worried about the fluctuations in the UK's economic growth. When the UK's economy starts to expand, problems of inflation and balance of payments tend to develop and government action to counter the problems often puts a brake on economic activity.

Table 4 shows a comparison of the UK's economic growth rate with those of five other countries. In the early periods UK growth was slow relative to those countries. This was also true in the early 1990s. However, the period 1995–97 saw the UK growth rate rise and overtake those of Germany, France, Italy and Japan.

Table 4 Changes in real GDP per annum

	UK	Germany	France	Italy	USA	Japan
1960–68	3.2	4.2	5.5	5.8	4.5	10.2
1968–73	3.4	5.0	5.5	4.5	3.0	8.8
1975–79	1.3	2.5	3.0	4.0	2.6	3.8
1979–90	2.5	2.4	2.5	2.7	2.7	4.4
1990–94	1.2	1.8	1.2	1.2	2.3	1.5
1995–97	3.0	1.6	2.0	1.7	3.3	2.7

Sources: *Economics Today*, November 1995; and *National Institute Economic Review*, January 1999.

Causes of the UK's relative slow growth

A number of reasons are given for why the UK economy has tended to grow more slowly than many of its rivals. Most of these relate to the slower increase in output per worker resulting mainly from lower rates of increases in the quantity and quality of capital goods.

Lack of quantity and quality of capital investment

The UK has tended to devote fewer of its resources to investment than its rivals. This has meant that its workers have been operating with a lower quantity of capital equipment.

There has also been a lack of spending on research and development, and not all of the spending has been very productive. Government R&D has tended to concentrate on glamour projects such as nuclear physics and astrophysics rather than more commercial projects. Whilst the UK has a good record of inventions it performs less well on innovation.

The quality of investment has suffered not only from a lack of spending on R&D but also from the direction of investment. The UK has not always undertaken the most appropriate nor the most productive investment. Firms have invested in industries producing goods and services that are not experiencing increasing world demand and which have low productivity. The relatively low extra output gained from extra units of capital generates less profit and so less finance to invest. This has led to a **vicious circle** of uncompetitiveness and low growth.

The low quality of investment has also affected the standard of goods and services produced. Relatively poor quality of goods and services, combined sometimes with poor marketing and after-sales service, has meant that income elasticity of demand for exports has been low while the income elasticity of demand for imports has been high.

Stop–go cycles

The UK faces a **balance-of-payments constraint.** As incomes grow more imports are 'sucked' into the economy. This tendency has resulted in a vicious circle developing with periods of expansion followed by periods of deflationary fiscal and monetary policy (the **stop–go cycle**) made necessary by a crisis in the balance of payments.

Lack of investment in human capital

The proportion of 16–18 year olds who stay on in education is higher in most other European countries, and the quality of UK secondary education has been compared unfavourably with a variety of countries including some in the Far East. It is also claimed that too much

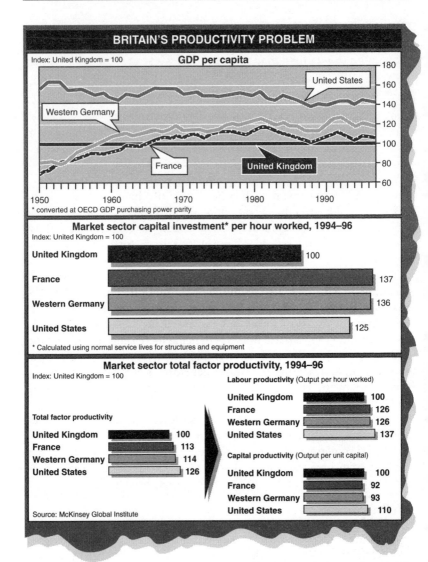

BRITAIN'S PRODUCTIVITY PROBLEM

GDP per capita
Index: United Kingdom = 100

* converted at OECD GDP purchasing power parity

Market sector capital investment* per hour worked, 1994–96
Index: United Kingdom = 100

United Kingdom	100
France	137
Western Germany	136
United States	125

* Calculated using normal service lives for structures and equipment

Market sector total factor productivity, 1994–96
Index: United Kingdom = 100

Total factor productivity

United Kingdom	100
France	113
Western Germany	114
United States	126

Labour productivity (Output per hour worked)

United Kingdom	100
France	126
Western Germany	126
United States	137

Capital productivity (Output per unit capital)

United Kingdom	100
France	92
Western Germany	93
United States	110

Source: McKinsey Global Institute

The Times, 3 November 1998

emphasis is given to education in the humanities at the expense of education in science and technology.

The availability of part-time education is greater in most other European countries. The percentage of public expenditure devoted to vocational training in the UK is low by standards of the European Union and adult literacy levels compare unfavourably. Employer spending on training is also low. This results in skill shortages, particularly during boom periods. Low skill levels may encourage firms to adopt low-technology processes which then require lower skill levels and less training – another vicious circle.

The clipping from *The Times*, 'Britain's productivity problem' (page 48), shows the productivity gap between Britain and some of its main rivals. The gap is particularly noticeable in relation to the USA.

Poor labour relations

The UK now has a relatively low strike rate. However, there is still evidence that an improvement in relations between managers and workers would raise productivity.

Collective bargaining remains fragmented, with different unions operating in the same industry and the same workplace. Less fragmented collective bargaining structures in Germany and Japan, with more single unions, have contributed to greater employee consultation at firm level in these countries. In the UK, labour relations could be improved not only by an increase in consultation but also by, for example, the development of a 'no-blame' culture.

In addition, job rotation and crèche facilities, for example, might increase labour flexibility and motivation.

Finance

Japanese and German banks are more likely to be represented on supervisory boards and perform long-term services (e.g. as a monitor of managerial performance). UK firms pay a higher proportion of their profits as dividends to shareholders than many of their rivals. As a result firms have less of their profits available for investment research and training. The low gearing (i.e. relatively small proportion of finance obtained from loans compared with shares) also increases the cost of finance. This is because it is expected that higher returns will be paid to shareholders than to creditors.

Short-termism

Short-termism comes in two forms. Firstly, UK firms tend to concentrate on short-term profitability. This is partly to keep their shareholders happy and partly to avoid the threat of takeover. Managers do not devote sufficient funds to long-term research and development. Secondly, UK governments have been criticized for pursuing short-term objectives and frequently changing policy approaches and instruments.

Stage of development

Some economists, including Nicholas Kaldor and Charles Kindleberger, have claimed that the UK and USA grow slowly because they have a high proportion of their workforce in the service sector. They believe that the scope for increases in productivity through technological advance is greater in the manufacturing than in the service sector.

Cultural attitudes

Some claim that cultural attitudes in the UK mitigate against economic growth. It is argued that graduates are not attracted to manufacturing. It is also claimed that there is widespread resistance to change among managers, workers and educationalists.

The extract from the *Sunday Times* brings together many of the causes of Britain's competitiveness gap.

Causes of Britain's competitiveness gap

Andrew Lorenz and David Smith

- The education system reinforces cultural bias against industry.
- Top talent spurns industry for the City and other professions.
- Obsession with process stifles entrepreneurialism.
- Both service and manufacturing sectors suffer from lack of the competition that spurs productivity growth in other countries.
- Big companies are under-represented in high-growth sectors relative to other Group of Seven (G7) countries.
- Front-line managers in industry are paid much less than their German or American counterparts.

- Britain has a consultancy-dominated culture which discourages development of hands-on management skills.
- Investment in automation and information technology lags behind European and American rivals.
- Lack of innovation spending means UK is deficient in new product development.
- Britain falls between two stools. Americans have economies of scale; French and Germans make more robust, higher quality products.

Sunday Times, 11 October 1998

Contrasts between developed and developing countries' growth rates

Growth rates vary between developing economies, with some having very high rates. Mishan, a well known critic of economic growth, and other economists have also claimed that if the shortcomings in the measuring of GDP were acknowledged and adjustments were made for them, living standards in the west would compare less favourably with those in developing countries.

However, using conventional GDP figures, developed countries have, in the main, higher and more stable rates of economic growth than developing ones. A number of explanations are advanced for the relatively slow growth rate of some developing countries. These include:

- *Inappropriate government policies.* Some economists argue that there are economic opportunities for developing countries, but policies which would permit full advantage to be taken of these opportunities are not adopted.
- *The under-development trap.* Poor countries can find it difficult to move out of poverty. They have a low level of capital per worker. This results in low productivity and low incomes. The low incomes mean that saving levels and capital accumulation are low – a vicious circle of poverty (Figure 12).
- *High population growth.* The increase in the labour force is usually more than outweighed by the increase in the dependency rate and the proportion of capital devoted to, for example, schools, hospitals and roads. The growth in population often exceeds the growth in capital, leading to a fall in the capital/labour ratio.

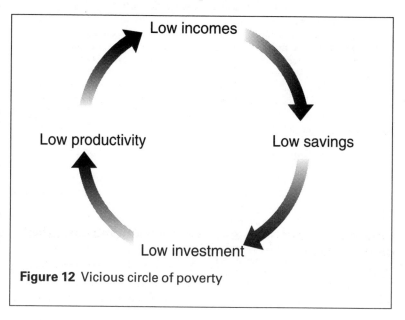

Figure 12 Vicious circle of poverty

- *International indebtedness.* Developing countries borrow in an attempt to increase their economic development. However, if the loans do not generate a flow of income in excess of the debt repayments the countries will get into further debt. Indeed in some years there is net outward flow of funds from developing countries to developed countries in the form of debt repayments.

Much ado about openness

[Few] doubt that freer trade helps poor countries grow faster. That may be conventional wisdom, but free-trade aficionados have not won the day entirely. Economists are still busy trying to understand whether, and how, free trade boosts economic growth. More worryingly, the IMF, which specializes in designing economic reforms for poor countries, turns out to have been remarkably unambitious in pushing openness.

Does free trade really matter? Strange though it may seem, this widely accepted proposition has not been easy to prove incontrovertibly. It is clear that lowering trade barriers delivers an economic shot in the arm as inefficiencies are eliminated. But this is different from showing that trade leads to a higher rate of growth in the long run.

On the contrary, traditional economic models posit that liberalization delivers a one-time gain, after which the economy will grow at the same rate as before. The connection between trade and growth rates has also been hard to prove empirically. Although there is no lack of anecdotal evidence that countries open to trade grow faster – think only of Chile, Hong Kong or Singapore – isolating the impact of lowered trade barriers is tricky. Trade can be restricted in numerous ways, from tariffs and quotas to less obvious measures, such as foreign-exchange controls. A careful measure of trade liberalization needs to quantify all these diverse restrictions, a difficult task.

Most studies have tried to solve this problem by using simpler measures of openness. However, the focus of Sebastian Edwards, of the University of California, is 'total factor productivity' (TFP), which measures how efficiently an economy puts both capital and labour to use. This makes sense, because all economists agree that a country's rate of economic growth depends on the accumulation of capital and labour and on increases in the productivity with which they are used.

As Mr Edwards looks at it, a country's TFP growth can have two different sources, domestic innovation or technological advances imported from abroad. The rate of domestic innovation depends on the country's stock of human capital – in other words, of creative, educated workers. Imported innovation is more important to poorer countries, where human capital is generally scarcer. Innovation may be introduced through imported goods and services. If this model is correct, the speed with which a poorer country improves its TFP relative to more advanced countries should depend partly upon how eagerly it welcomes such imports – in other words, how open it is to trade.

The Economist, 21 March 1998

Ways to increase the growth rates of developing countries

Again a number of suggestions are advanced.

More apt foreign aid

Developing countries prefer untied multilateral aid at low rates of interest. Tied, bilateral aid may require developing countries to undertake projects they do not consider appropriate and to buy capital and raw materials from not necessarily the most appropriate sources.

Increase productivity in agriculture

For a number of developing countries, with large agricultural sectors, this may prove to be the easiest and quickest way to promote growth. Relatively cheap and staged improvements could be made in terms of, say, equipment, irrigation and fertilizers. The same level of prior technical knowledge and capital investment would not be required as would be necessary to increase productivity in manufacturing.

Population control

This would reduce the pressure of population on resources and permit capital accumulation to occur at a faster rate.

Increased aggregate demand

As we have seen, this would be likely to increase output in the short run but for economic growth to continue there must also be an increase in the productive potential of the economy.

Freer international trade

Developing countries experience tariffs and other restrictions imposed by major trading blocs, including the EU, which makes it difficult for them to sell their goods. Some economists and politicians in developed countries are concerned about the 'threat imposed by low wage economies'. However this misses the whole point of comparative advantage (see the article from *The Economist*, page 52).

KEY WORDS

Black economy
Regrettables
Purchasing power parities
Human development index
Headline indicators of the
     quality of life

Vicious circle
Balance of payments constraint
Stop–go cycle
Short-termism

Further reading

Ball, J., Chapter 2 in *The British Economy at the Crossroads*, FT/Pitman Publishing, 1998.

Beardshaw, J. *et al.*, *Economics: A Student's Guide*, 4th edn, Addison-Wesley Longman, 1998.

Grant, S., Chapter 55 in *Stanlake's Introductory Economics*, 7th edn, Addison-Wesley Longman, 1999.

Nixson, F., Chapter 10 in *Development Economics*, Heinemann Educational, 1996.

Useful websites

World Bank: www.worldbank.org/prospects/gep
EU: www.rcade.essex.ac.uk

Essay topics

1. (a) Explain how you would attempt to measure the extent to which the living standards of citizens of different countries vary. [12 marks]

   (b) Discuss the difficulties which are likely to be encountered in attempting to construct and interpret such indicators to obtain an accurate reflection of differences in living standards. [13 marks]
   [Associated Examining Board, 1998]

2. Analyse the causes of the UK's slow growth rate. [25 marks]

Data response question

This task is based on a question set by the University of London Examinations and Assessment Council in 1998. Study all the data given on the UK's economic performance in relation to other major economies, and then answer the questions that follow.

Table A Where the UK stands: GDP per person

Rank	1979	1994
1	USA	Luxembourg
2	Switzerland	USA
3	Luxembourg	Switzerland
4	Canada	Japan
5	France	Belgium
6	Sweden	Norway
7	Iceland	Denmark
8	Netherlands	Canada

Rank	1979	1994
9	Denmark	Iceland
10	Austria	Austria
11	Australia	France
12	Belgium	Germany
13	**UK**	Italy
14	Germany	Netherlands
15	Italy	Australia
16	Norway	Hong Kong
17	Japan	Singapore
18	New Zealand	**UK**

Source: *The Guardian*, 2 November 1995.

Table B Where the UK stands: consumer prices (% change)

Rank	1979	1995
1	Switzerland (3.6)	Japan (-0.4)
2	Japan (3.7)	Iceland (1.4)
3	Austria (3.7)	Switzerland (1.6)
4	Germany (4.1)	Finland (1.7)
5	Netherlands (4.2)	Belgium (1.7)
6	Luxembourg (4.5)	France (1.8)
7	Belgium (4.5)	Canada (2.2)
8	Norway (4.8)	Luxembourg (2.3)
9	Sweden (7.2)	Netherlands (2.3)
10	Finland (7.5)	Germany (2.3)
11	Australia (9.1)	Austria (2.4)
12	Canada (9.1)	Denmark (2.5)
13	Denmark (9.6)	Ireland (2.5)
14	France (10.8)	Sweden (2.6)
15	USA (11.3)	Norway (2.7)
16	Ireland (13.2)	USA (2.9)
17	**UK (13.4)**	**UK (3.5)**
18	New Zealand (13.8)	Australia (3.9)

Source: As for Table A.

Table C Where the UK stands: unemployment rates (% of population)

Rank	1979*	1995†
1	Norway (2.0)	Japan (3.1)
2	Japan (2.1)	Norway (5.2)
3	Sweden (2.1)	USA (5.6)
4	Germany (3.2)	New Zealand (6.3)
5	**UK (5.0)**	Netherlands (6.7)
6	Netherlands (5.4)	Portugal (7.2)
7	USA (5.8)	Germany (8.1)
8	France (5.8)	Australia (8.3)
9	Finland (5.9)	**UK (8.8)**
10	Australia (6.2)	Sweden (9.1)
11	Canada (7.4)	Canada (9.5)
12	Italy (7.6)	Belgium (9.8)
13	Belgium (8.2)	France (11.6)
14	Spain (8.4)	Italy (12.2)
15		Ireland (14.5)
16		Finland (17.6)
17		Spain (22.5)

* No figures for Ireland, New Zealand, Portugal and Switzerland.
† No figure for Switzerland.
Source: As for Table A.

Figure A Change in real GDP: volume index, 1995 (1985 = 100)

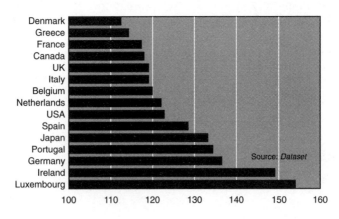

Source: *Dataset*

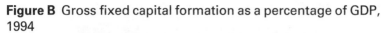

Figure B Gross fixed capital formation as a percentage of GDP, 1994

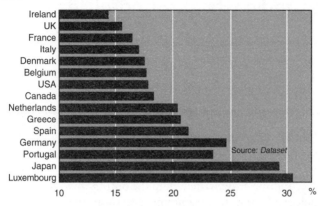

1. (a) Examine Tables A, B and C. What do these data indicate about the state of the economy in the UK compared with Japan in 1994/95? [6 marks]
   (b) Identify *two* other pieces of information from these tables which would help you to make a more accurate assessment of the state of the UK and Japanese economies. Explain their significance. [4 marks]
2. (a) Define the phrase 'change in real GDP: volume index 1995 (1985 = 100)' as used in Figure A. [3 marks]
   (b) With reference to Figure B, examine the economic significance of the different proportions of GDP devoted to gross fixed capital formation in the UK and Luxembourg in 1994. [6 marks]
3. Examine the problems in comparing changes in living standards over time. [6 marks]

Chapter Five

Benefits and costs of economic growth

'Understanding growth is surely the most urgent task in economics.
Across the world, poverty remains the single greatest cause of misery
and the surest remedy for poverty is economic growth.'
The Economist, 25 May 1996

Economic growth can have a number of effects on an economy, some beneficial and some harmful. The net impact will largely depend on the nature of the economic growth, including the output mix and how the growth is achieved, and the economic situation of the country.

For example, sustainable economic growth is clearly more desirable than economic growth achieved as a result of the depletion of non-renewable resources.

Perception of economic growth

The need for economic growth is questioned more in developed countries than in developing ones. When living standards are already high in a country some may consider that the potential costs of growth may exceed the potential benefits. Indeed some politicians and economists, concerned particularly about the effects on the environment, advocate a policy of **zero economic growth**.

However, as the quote at the beginning of the chapter suggests, in those countries where the output produced is currently insufficient to house, feed and educate the population, it is generally accepted that there is no alternative but to increase output.

So some developing countries see economic growth as a necessity. Even in developed countries most people, desiring higher living standards, welcome economic growth.

Benefits of economic growth

● Higher living standards

The main benefit of economic growth is thought to be higher material living standards. Increases in output create the opportunity for people to enjoy more goods and more services.

As incomes rise people are able to spend a smaller proportion of their income on necessities and a higher proportion on luxury goods. Whereas, for example, 60 per cent of UK household expenditure went on food in 1914, the proportion spent had fallen to 25 per cent in 1974, 16.7 per cent in 1987 and 13 per cent by 1998. The proportion spent on leisure goods and services, which were first measured as items separate from personal goods and services in 1987, continues to rise. In 1987 it was 8 per cent and by 1998 it was 10.5 per cent.

With higher incomes and more goods and services available, people have more choice on how to spend their leisure time.

Higher incomes permit people to enjoy more consumer durables. According to the 1998 *General Household Survey*, 98 per cent of UK households had a television, 94 per cent had a telephone, 92 per cent had a washing machine and 90 per cent had central heating. These figures compare with 93, 42, 66 and 37 per cent respectively in 1972.

Table 5 shows how possession of a video recorder has increased among all types of households between 1986 and 1996/97.

Table 5 Households with a video recorder: by socioeconomic group, 1986 and 1996/97 (percentages)

	1986	*1996/97*
Professional	50	91
Employers and managers	61	95
Intermediate non-manual	45	92
Junior non-manual	47	91
Skilled manual	55	94
Semi-skilled manual	45	89
Unskilled manual	34	86
Economically inactive	14	66
All socioeconomic groups	38	82

Source: ONS, *Social Trends* 28, Table 13.5, 1998.

Economic growth can potentially change material living standards at a significant rate. For example in the UK output has increased by 80 per cent in real terms since 1970.

● Increased life expectancy

Improvements in nutrition, sanitation, heating, healthcare and working conditions enable people to live longer. Table 6 shows how life expectancy has increased over the twentieth century in England and Wales.

Table 6 Life expectancy at birth in England and Wales, by gender, from 1901 to 1996

	1901	1971	1976	1981	1985	1991	1994	1996
Males	45.3	69.0	70.0	71.1	71.9	73.4	74.3	74.6
Females	49.2	75.2	76.1	77.1	77.6	78.9	79.6	79.7

Source: ONS, *Social Trends 28,* Table 7.2, 1998.

● Reduction in poverty

Economic growth also enables a government to alleviate poverty. Higher incomes will increase tax revenue and some of this can be used to fund programmes to reduce poverty. In the absence of economic growth a government would have to reduce the incomes of the rich in order to help the poor. However, whilst it does mean that absolute poverty is reduced it does not necessarily mean that relative poverty will be reduced.

● Improved public services

Higher tax revenues generated as a result of economic growth can also be used to improve the level and quality of public sector educational and health service provision. More students can continue into higher education and more ailments can be treated. The resulting improvement in the quality of the labour force will in turn increase productivity capacity.

● Reduction in pollution

Some of the revenue may be spent on cleaning up the environment. If productive capacity increases, it may be possible to improve the environment without forgoing other goods and services. Some economists argue that as people become richer they also become more concerned about the quality of the environment and more willing for resources to be devoted to protecting it. Indeed there is a debate about whether economic growth leads to an improvement or a deterioration in the environment. The outcome will depend on how the growth is achieved and how the extra output produced is employed.

● Meet expectations of improved living standards

Economic growth can enable peoples' expectations of rising living standards to be met. If output does not rise but aggregate demand increases, problems of inflation and balance of payments difficulties will occur. There may also be a deterioration in labour relations as workers and employers fight over an unchanging level of output.

● Increased status

Economic growth can raise the status and influence of a country. Voting rights at the International Monetary Fund (IMF), for example, depend in part on the size of a country's GDP. As China has experienced faster economic growth its influence in world affairs has increased.

The following article from the *Independent on Sunday* questions the benefits of economic growth.

Is today really so much better?

DAVID NICHOLSON-LORD

What we do know, through opinion surveys, is that there appears to be no relationship between contentment and GDP. Polls by the University of Chicago since the 1950s have shown that, despite four decades of affluence, people do not find themselves any happier: levels of general satisfaction with life have actually fallen.

Yet if the evidence suggests things may be getting worse, is economic growth responsible? Isn't it too broad a concept to blame, say, for the breakdown in family life? If growth simply means more things, there is no reason why it should make life better: it is a quantitative, not a qualitative, target. More calories, beyond the point where they meet nutritional needs standards, translate into obesity. More money may mean more capacity to kill oneself with cigarettes or fast cars. More goods turn into more litter, rubbish, pollution, loss of land and natural resources. Clearly, part of the issue is what we use the growth to achieve.

One overriding purpose has been the promotion of convenience and choice through technology. Yet every piece of gadgetry has a dark side. … The enormous hidden costs of the car are now being appreciated. But what about such apparent triumphs as television, the telephone and central heating? Americans spend 20 hours a week – half their spare time – watching television: is this an active, discriminating, neighbourly use of leisure? And has the telephone promoted or compensated for the geographical separation of family and friends? … Central heating has contributed to an asthma epidemic – humid and unventilated houses are potent breeding grounds for asthma allergies – as well as making us more prone to coughs and colds. It has also helped to prise apart family life: think of how teenagers treat their bedrooms as self-contained flatlets.

Independent on Sunday, 3 January 1993

Costs of economic growth
● Opportunity cost

There may be an **opportunity cost of economic growth**. To increase output more resources have to be devoted to the production of capital goods. If a country is using all of its resources this can be achieved only by a reduction in the output of consumer goods. Figure 13 shows a country switching resources from consumer to capital goods. The opportunity cost of producing an extra 150 capital goods is 200 consumer goods.

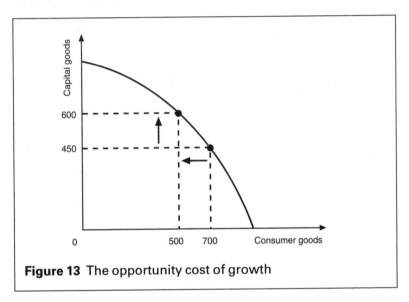

Figure 13 The opportunity cost of growth

To finance the investment in capital goods, either saving or taxation has to increase – which is why consumption falls. However, the opportunity cost is only a short-term cost. When the extra capital goods are made the production possibility curve will move out to the right, and when they are put into use the output of consumer goods will increase.

If there are *unemployed resources* there may not be any opportunity cost, or there may be only a small opportunity cost even in the short run.

● Damage to the environment

A major risk imposed by economic growth is that it may be achieved at the price of a deterioration in the environment. Higher production and consumption levels will put pressure on natural resources – including non-renewable resources such as fossil fuels – and may generate higher levels of noise, air and water pollution and increased risk of ecological disasters.

● Social stresses
Economic growth may also create social stresses. A dynamic economy requires people and institutions to be adaptable, but some people may find this difficult to cope with. For example, workers may be required to move from one area of the country to another, to switch occupations and to keep up with changes in working methods and changes in technology. The pace of work may increase. Income may become less evenly distributed. Some will do well but others may feel left behind. This is likely to have consequences for crime rates, mental health problems, divorce and other social problems.

● Deterioration in the quality of life
Whilst economic growth enables more resources to be devoted to healthcare with the result that more ailments can be treated, it is thought it may also give rise to other medical problems. For example, the increased use of central heating has been associated with a rise in the number of asthma sufferers. The increased use of the car has also resulted in more deaths, accidents and breathing-related illnesses. In addition, as mentioned above there may be more stress-related illnesses.

As output increases people are living longer but it is not just length of life which is important but also the quality of life. Table 7 indicates that healthy life expectancy did not improve between 1991 and 1994.

Table 7 Healthy life expectancy at birth in England and Wales, by gender, from 1976 to 1994

	1976	1981	1985	1991	1994
Males	58.3	58.7	58.8	59.9	59.2
Females	62.0	61.0	61.9	63.0	62.2

Source: Table 7.2, ONS, *Social Trends* 28, 1998.

● Poverty
As noted above, economic growth can enable more resources to be devoted to reducing poverty. Unfortunately it also has the potential to make life more difficult for the poor and may increase relative poverty.

The importance of economic growth in developing countries

Understanding growth is surely the most urgent task in economics. Across the world, poverty remains the single greatest cause of misery; and the surest remedy for poverty is economic growth. It is true that growth can create problems of its own (congestion and pollution, for instance), which may preoccupy many people in rich countries. But such ills pale in comparison with the harm caused by the economic backwardness of poor countries – that is, of the larger part of the world. The cost of this backwardness, measured in wasted lives and needless suffering, is truly vast.

To its shame, economics neglected the study of growth for many years. Theorists and empirical researchers alike chose to concentrate on other fields, notably on macroeconomic policy. Until the 1980s, with a few exceptions, the best brains in economics preferred not to focus on the most vital issue of all. But over the past ten years or so, this has changed. Stars such as Robert Lucas of the University of Chicago, who last year won the Nobel Prize in economics, have started to concentrate on growth. As he says of the subject, 'the consequences for human welfare … are simply staggering. Once one starts to think about them, it is hard to think of anything else.'

The Economist, 25 May 1996

As incomes increase some resources will be shifted from making cheap products to making more luxury items. Those unable to afford to run a car may increasingly be excluded from leisure facilities and hypermarkets. Growing economies may witness an increasing gap between the rich and the poor (see the above article from *The Economist*).

● Reduction in happiness

It is also claimed that having more goods and services does not necessarily make people happier. Indeed it is thought that growth merely generates extra demands.

Five years ago most households would have been content with, say, one personal computer, but now many households want one for every adult and for every school-age child.

Some of the goods and services purchased may be bought merely to cope with the problems caused by the type of lifestyle which exists in a growing economy, e.g. commuter transport.

The consumption of certain goods and services, sometimes referred to as **positional goods**, can be subject to absolute limitations in supply. For example, whilst economic growth has made foreign travel possible for more people it has reduced the number of 'unspoilt' and uncrowded holiday resorts.

Consumption is also subject to **diminishing returns**. The more we have, the less we appreciate extra units.

Influences on whether countries seek to aim for economic growth
These include:

- the current GDP level
- the relative benefits and costs involved
- the importance the population attaches to them
- the extent to which the costs and benefits can be affected.

Most countries, both developing and developed, seek to achieve economic growth whilst also seeking to avoid the potential harmful effects of growth by, for example, passing environmental protection legislation and signing up to international agreements limiting the burning of fossil fuels.

KEY WORDS

Zero economic growth   Positional goods
Opportunity cost of economic   Diminishing returns
  growth

Further reading
Anderton, A., Unit 100 in *Economics*, 2nd edn, Causeway Press, 1995.
Grant, S., Chapter 55 in *Stanlake's Introductory Economics*, 7th edn, Longman, 1997.
Mackintosh, M. *et al.*, Chapter 27 in *Economics and Changing Economies*, Open University Press, 1996.
Maunder, P., Myers, D., Wall, N. and Miller, R., Chapter 26 in *Economics Explained*, 3rd edn, Collins Educational, 1995.

Useful websites
UN Statistics Division: www.un.org/depts/unsd/
Financial Times: www.ft.com/

Essay topics
1. (a) Explain what is meant by an increase in the rate of economic growth. [5 marks]

(b) Assess the possible benefits and costs of an increase in a country's rate of economic growth. [20 marks]

2. (a) Explain why a developed economy is more likely to question the benefits of economic growth than a developing economy. [10 marks]

(b) Discuss how a developing country could seek to increase its growth rate. [15 marks]

Data response question

Read the following article from *The Sunday Times* of 6 December 1998 (by Cherry Norton, with additional reporting by Karen Bayne). Then answer the questions that follow.

Richer Britain gets depressed

The old adage is true: money really can't buy you happiness. A study has shown that Britons get less enjoyment and happiness from their money than most other nations.

The research into the link between personal spending power and the perceived quality of life showed that Bangladesh citizens, in one of the poorest countries in the world, get far more happiness from their small incomes than the British do from their relatively large ones. Britain also lags behind the Philippines, Nigeria and Ghana, and is placed thirty-second out of the 54 countries measured [see Table A].

'People in Britain are generally less happy than they were 10 years ago. Two-thirds would rather see the environment improved than have more economic growth and personal spending money,' said Robert Worcester, visiting professor of government at the London School of Economics, who co-wrote the study.

The study by Demos, the independent think tank, shows that although the British have twice as much money to spend in real terms compared with 40 years ago, their perceived quality of life has not improved. Earlier studies have shown that many Britons still believe that money does bring happiness. The Demos research shows that such a link still exists in poor countries because a small increase in income can mean large improvements in lifestyle.

However, above a certain level of income that direct relationship breaks down and, the research suggests, happiness in Britain is far more dependent on close personal relationships, good health and job satisfaction.

The researchers concluded that although Britons are rich compared

Table A World happiness survey: level of happiness once income is taken into account

	Country		Country		Country
1	Bangladesh	19	Argentina	37	France
2	Azerbaijan	20	Hungary	38	Norway
3	Nigeria	21	Estonia	39	Austria
4	Philippines	22	Armenia	40	Portugal
5	India	23	South Korea	41	Switzerland
6	Ghana	24	Chile	42	Germany
7	Georgia	25	Romania	43	Canada
8	China	26	Ireland	44	Japan
9	Poland	27	Sweden	45	Italy
10	Turkey	28	Czech Rep.	46	United States
11	Dominican Rep.	29	Netherlands	47	Slovenia
12	South Africa	30	Australia	48	Lithuania
13	Venezuela	31	Spain	49	Slovakia
14	Brazil	**32**	**Britain**	50	Russia
15	Uruquay	33	Finland	51	Ukraine
16	Latvia	34	Iceland	52	Belarus
17	Croatia	35	Denmark	53	Bulgaria
18	Mexico	36	Belgium	54	Moldova

with most other countries, many suffer from an emotional poverty caused by consumerism and the destruction of communities.

For many people, the research will only confirm their decision to 'downshift' by exchanging affluent lifestyles for ones that allow more time for personal interests.

1. By how much does the article suggest the British economy grew between 1958 and 1998? [2 marks]
2. 'Two-thirds would rather see the environment improved than have more economic growth.' Discuss whether economic growth and improvements in the environment are conflicting objectives. [6 marks]
3. Why may the effects of an increase in income differ between a developing and a developed country? [6 marks]
4. What 'personal needs' may not be met by economic growth? [6 marks]
5. How does the UK's level of happiness compare with the other EU countries included in the table? [5 marks]

Chapter Six

Economic growth and government policy

'The government's central economic objective is to achieve high and stable levels of growth and employment so that everyone in Britain can share in higher living standards and greater job opportunities.'
Pre-budget 1998; a pocket guide, HM Treasury, November 1997

Influences on government policy
The measures a government may adopt to promote and influence economic growth will depend on:

- how beneficial it believes economic growth is
- what it believes are the key determinants of economic growth
- the rate it is aiming for
- the effects the measures will have on its other objectives.

Macroeconomic objectives
As we saw in the previous chapter, most countries want to achieve economic growth. They also want steady increases in output. This is because stable economic growth enables firms and individuals to plan ahead and avoids the costs which can be encountered when economic activity swings from boom to slump (e.g. liquidations and negative equity).

Stable economic growth is only one of the four major macroeconomic objectives. The other three are (a) low inflation, (b) full employment, and (c) a balance of payments equilibrium. Both economic growth and employment tend to benefit, at least in the short run, from reflationary policies which increase aggregate demand. However, such policies may contribute to inflation and cause balance of payments difficulties. To avoid this conflict of objectives a government may seek to achieve long-run economic growth by stimulating both aggregate demand and aggregate supply.

Policy approaches
- **Keynesian policies**
Keynesian economists tend to favour an interventionist and demand-

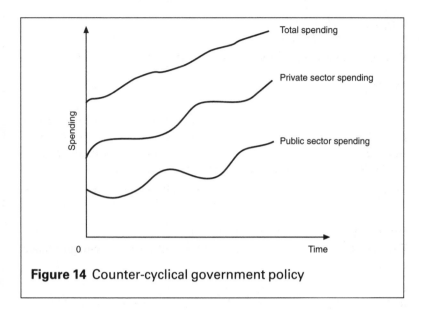

Figure 14 Counter-cyclical government policy

side approach. They believe that the economy is inherently unstable and that without government intervention there may be considerable fluctuations in economic activity. So they advocate that in order to achieve stable economic growth the government should act **counter-cyclically**, increasing aggregate demand by raising government spending and/or cutting taxation when private sector spending is low and reducing aggregate demand when private sector spending is too high.

Figure 14 shows a government acting counter-cyclically by altering its spending to offset the fluctuations in private sector spending.

Deliberate manipulation of the level of aggregate demand by the government is known as **active (or discretionary) demand management**. Slight adjustments to the level of aggregate demand to achieve precise levels of GDP and employment is known as **fine-tuning**. Nowadays most Keynesians recognize that governments have to aim for **coarse-tuning**. This means seeking to move the economy in the desired direction rather than seeking to hit precise targets.

By ensuring that aggregate demand does not fluctuate unduly but instead rises at a smooth rate, Keynesians believe that the government will encourage firms to invest and thereby increase the potential output of the economy and hence the trend growth rate.

● New classical policies

New classical economists favour a market-orientated and supply-side approach. They believe that market failure is not a significant problem and that the private sector is inherently stable over the long run. They think that if left to market forces, resources will move to reflect changes in consumer demand. They believe that entrepreneurs, driven by the profit motive to respond to consumer demand, are the best judges of what to produce and how to produce it.

They also think there is a high risk of government failure, with government intervention resulting in less efficient allocation of resources because of lack of information, **time lags** and because government measures may reduce the flexibility of wages and prices. So they support measures to promote economic growth which reduce government intervention, increase the incentives for private sector entrepreneurs to increase investment and output and the unemployed to seek work more actively.

Free market policies like privatization and trade union reform, they argue, will increase long-run aggregate supply and raise output, as shown in Figure 15.

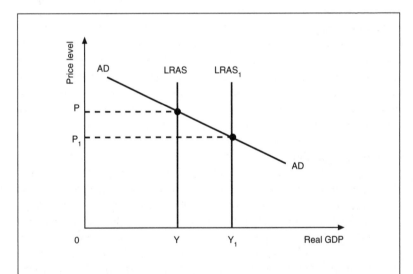

Figure 15 The effect of an increase in long-run aggregate supply (new classical approach)

- ● Automatic stabilizers

Some forms of government spending and taxation change automatically in terms of their levels with the business cycle and in such a way as to mitigate the fluctuations.

When, for example, the economy is moving towards recession, government spending on job seekers' allowance will automatically increase as there will be more people unemployed. Tax revenue from income tax and VAT will fall as there will be fewer people working, income levels will be lower and people will be spending less. Governments will permit these **automatic stabilizers** to operate by not changing tax rates or benefit levels.

However, governments may also seek to achieve economic growth by active policy measures that change, for example, income tax rates, increase research and development grants, lower interest rates and increase allowances against tax for investment and depreciation. It is active policy which is concentrated on below.

Examples of policy measures to promote economic growth

There is a range of policy measures which a government could adopt.

- ● Fiscal policy

As an example of **fiscal policy**, the government could stimulate aggregate demand by raising government spending and/or cutting taxation. This will increase actual growth at least in the short run if there is initially spare capacity, but its effects on long-run growth will depend on how economic agents react to the changes and – in the case of government spending – what the spending goes on.

- ● Monetary policy

As an example of **monetary policy**, increasing the money supply, cutting interest rates and lowering the exchange rate will also increase aggregate demand. A country which operates an independent exchange rate system could reduce the value of its exchange rate to promote demand for its goods and services, and thereby generate output. However, this will raise the costs of imports and may contribute to cost-push inflation. Lower interest rates should also increase investment and thereby increase aggregate supply in the long run.

- ● Supply-side policy

Supply-side policy measures, as their name suggests, seek to increase long-run aggregate supply.

To encourage entrepreneurs to expand their output, new classical economists urge measures which reduce government interference in their activities and which increase their financial incentives. For example, they support measures which reduce government red tape and lower corporation tax. They also advocate measures which will reduce the natural rate of unemployment by increasing the gap between income from employment and the income the unemployed receive from the state. The main measures they propose to achieve this are cutting income tax and cutting job-seekers' allowance.

Keynesians do not support reducing the job-seekers' allowance as they do not believe that most of the unemployed are involuntarily unemployed. However, they do support measures which increase long-run aggregate supply by raising the quality of resources through promoting increases in investment in human and physical capital (see the following boxed item).

Promoting growth

The government is taking further steps to increase the sustainable rate of growth by raising productivity, increasing employment opportunity and building a fairer society.

Closing the productivity gap of approaching 40 per cent with the USA and over 20 per cent with France and Germany would help to increase growth, jobs and living standards. The UK has in the past invested in less:

- *research and development* (R&D): the US invests 50 per cent more as a share of GDP than the UK in business R&D
- *new capital equipment*: investment per person is 40 per cent higher in Germany
- *the basic skill levels of the workforce*: 22 per cent of adults in the UK have poor literacy skills, 50 per cent more than in Germany.

Budget 99 delivers a better deal for business and enterprise. It builds on steps that have already been taken to: increase investment; promote innovation; strengthen competition; and improve skills:

- for small businesses, a new 10p corporation tax rate and 40 per cent capital allowances to encourage investment and growth
- a new research and development tax credit to encourage small business investment in R&D
- a new employee share ownership scheme to encourage employees to take a stake in the success of their companies
- a new small business service to support growing small firms
- big discounts from 2000 on training costs through individual learning accounts.

Source: Budget 99, HM Treasury, March 1999

Current UK government policy

The quote at the start of the chapter outlines the objectives, in terms of economic growth, of the Labour government elected in May 1997. It wants high growth, although it has not set a specific target for the growth rate figure.

As the boxed item on page 72 indicates, the main way it is seeking to raise long-run growth is through measures designed to increase productivity and hence productive potential. It is placing particular emphasis on education and training.

It also wants a stable growth rate. The main way it is seeking to achieve this is by making government policy itself more stable so that economic agents can plan ahead with more certainty and so that stop–go cycles can be avoided. Among the steps it has taken to achieve greater policy stability are:

- the adoption of the so-called Golden Rule which is that the government will, over the economic cycle, borrow only to finance public investment and not current public spending
- following a sustainable investment rule which states that the government has to keep public sector debt at a stable level over the economic cycle
- setting three-year spending plans for government departments
- transferring operational responsibility for interest rates to the Bank of England so that interest rates cannot be manipulated for electoral advantage.

Examples of government measures

In this section we will examine three possible measures in more detail.

● A reduction in interest rates

Lower interest rates will increase the discretionary income of those who have borrowed in the past, discourage saving and reduce the cost of buying on credit. Hence consumption is likely to increase. The measure may also increase aggregate demand by stimulating investment. Lower interest rates will reduce the cost of borrowing to invest and the opportunity cost of using retained profits for investment. An increase in investment is particularly significant. This is because it increases both aggregate demand and long-run aggregate supply. This is shown in Figure 16 from a Keynesian viewpoint (see also Figure 9 and its related text on pages 27 and 28).

A fall in interest rates may also stimulate economic growth via its impact on a floating exchange rate. Lower interest rates will be likely to

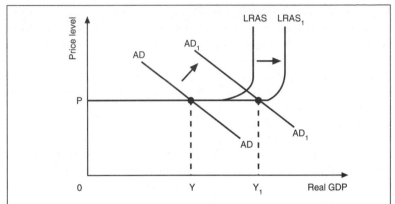

Figure 16 The effect of an increase in investment (Keynesian approach)

cause an outflow of hot money in search of higher returns abroad. The supply of sterling will increase, thereby reducing the value of the currency. A lower exchange rate will increase the price competitiveness of the country's goods and services at home and abroad. This will, at least in the short run, increase output.

However, a fall in interest rates may not have much impact on consumption and investment if households and entrepreneurs are pessimistic about the future. Keynesians argue that investment is relatively interest inelastic. They believe the main influence on investment is the expected yield. Interest rates may be cut, but if income and demand are falling firms are unlikely to want to invest.

The government has passed responsibility for setting the base interest rate to the Bank of England. In setting the interest rate the Bank of England's prime objective is to keep inflation low. However, it also takes into account the level of economic activity. If, and when, the UK joins the European single currency, responsibility for interest rate determination will pass to the European Central Bank.

● Increasing government spending
An increase in government expenditure will raise aggregate demand. According to Keynesians, if the economy is operating at less than full employment, the multiple rise in GDP will cause output and employment to rise.

However, according to new classical economists, an increase in aggregate demand will, in the long run, have no effect on output. As

Figure 17 shows, at first the rise in aggregate demand stimulates firms to expand and increase output. In doing this their costs rise, and when they realize that their real profit levels have not risen they cut their output back to the previous level. Similarly people attracted into the labour force by higher wages will leave the labour force when they understand that real wages have not risen. Output returns to its former level but at a higher price level.

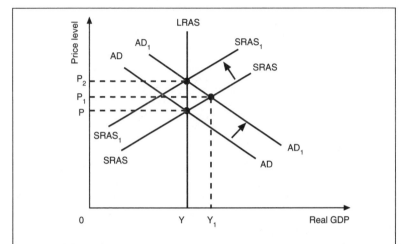

Figure 17 New classical view of an increase in government expenditure

● Cutting income tax

This will increase aggregate demand and may increase aggregate supply. A reduction in income tax will raise disposable income. This will increase consumption which in turn is likely to stimulate investment. However, the rise in consumer spending may not be very significant. This is because the main beneficiaries are likely to be high-income earners who have a relatively low marginal propensity to consume.

Income tax reductions are favoured by new classical economists. They argue that such cuts will result in a rise in the incentive to work and enterprise, thereby encouraging workers to work more hours, the unemployed to seek work more actively, and entrepreneurs to expand their interests. The resulting rise in employment and investment will shift the production possibility curve to the right.

To support their view of the benefits of cutting income tax rates,

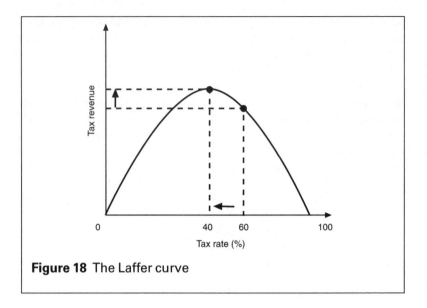

Figure 18 The Laffer curve

especially the high marginal rates, they make use of the **Laffer curve** (Figure 18). This suggests that a *cut in the rate* of income tax can – on the appropriate part of the curve, say from 60 to 40 per cent – actually

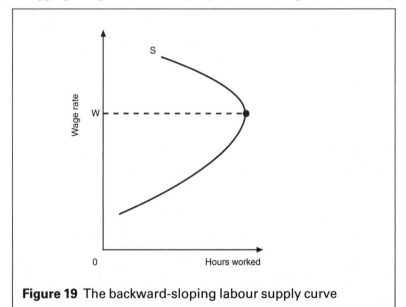

Figure 19 The backward-sloping labour supply curve

raise income tax revenue by increasing both actual economic activity and declared economic activity (there will be less incentive not to declare income to the tax authorities).

The Keynesians think the effects on aggregate supply are more uncertain. They believe that most unemployment is of an involuntary rather than voluntary nature. They also argue that most workers cannot alter the hours they work; and of those who can, about an equal number is likely to work *fewer* hours – since they can now afford more leisure time – as will work more hours.

The **backward-sloping labour supply curve** (Figure 19, page 76) suggests that once net wage rates reach a certain level, the *income effect* (causing workers to buy more leisure time) of further increases will be greater than the *substitution effect* (causing workers to substitute work for the now more expensive leisure) – and so less hours will be worked. On Figure 19, at a wage 0W the negative income effect outweighs the positive substitution effect.

Counter-cyclical policies

As noted above, governments aim for stable economic growth. However, there are risks behind employing demand management designed to counter fluctuations in economic activity. This is because of time lags. By the time it has been recognized that, say, private sector demand is starting to rise more slowly or even fall, and policy measures have been designed and introduced, then the level of economic activity may have changed. The economy may now be moving into the boom phase of a business cycle. If this is the case the government will be reinforcing rather than countering the cycle.

Stop–go cycles

Government policies can have the effect of reducing the rate and stability of economic growth if they are changed frequently. In the past, UK governments in particular have been criticized for engaging in stop–go policies which have contributed to the volatility of growth.

To promote economic growth a government might, for example, cut income tax revenue and it (or its central bank) may cut interest rates. These measures increase aggregate demand, with the multiplier and accelerator effects further increasing aggregate demand and output. However, if the higher aggregate demand results in inflation and/or a deficit on the current account of the balance of payments, a government may introduce measures to reduce aggregate demand. These would be likely to slow down the rate of economic activity.

KEY WORDS

Macroeconomic objectives
Counter-cyclically
Active/discretionary demand
   management
Fine-tuning
Coarse-tuning
Time lags

Automatic stabilizers
Fiscal policy
Monetary policy
Supply-side policy
Laffer curve
Backward-sloping labour
   supply curve

Further reading

Anderton, A., Unit 101 in *Economics*, 2nd edn, Causeway Press, 1995.

Healey, N. and Cook, M., Chapters 2, 5 and 6 in *Supply Side Economics*, 3rd edn, Heinemann Educational, 1996.

Mackintosh, M. *et al.*, Chapter 20 in *Economics and Changing Economies*, Open University Press, 1996.

Smith, D., Chapter 6 in *UK Current Economic Policy*, 2nd edn, Heinemann Educational, 1999.

Useful websites

HM Treasury: www.hm-treasury.gov.uk/
Bank of England: www.bankofengland.co.uk/

Essay topics

1. (a) Explain what is meant by economic growth. [3 marks]
   (b) Discuss *three* factors that determine the rate of growth within a country. [6 marks]
   (c) Evaluate two alternative macroeconomic policies that could be introduced to increase the rate of economic growth within a country. [11 marks] [University of Oxford Delegacy of Local Examinations 1997]
2. (a) Explain how an increase in government expenditure will lead to a higher level of national income. [12 marks]
   (b) Discuss whether raising government expenditure is the best way to achieve a sustained increase in national income. [13 marks] [University of Cambridge Local Examinations Syndicate 1998]

Data response question

This task is based on data from the UK National Accounts, *The Blue Book* (1998 edition), the *National Economic Review* (April 1999) and

The Monthly Digest of Statistics (May 1999). Study the data in the table, which shows the UK's and the Euro Area's growth rate for the period 1992 to 1998, and UK gross fixed capital formation divided into the categories of private and public sector investment. Then, using the data and your knowledge of economics, answer the questions that follow.

Table A Economic growth and investment

Year	Economic growth		UK investment at 1995 prices (£ million)	
	Growth rate of real GDP (%)		Private sector investment	Public sector investment
	UK	Euro Area		
1992	0.1	1.4	87 965	20 299
1993	2.3	–1.1	88 081	20 973
1994	4.4	2.6	91 753	21 289
1995	2.8	2.1	96 579	19 781
1996	2.6	1.7	106 137	15 905
1997	3.5	2.5	115 109	14 456
1998	2.1	2.9	123 497	13 557

1. (a) Briefly explain what is meant by real GDP. [1 mark]
   (b) Compare the UK's and the Euro Area's growth rate for the period shown. [2 marks]
2. (a) Discuss the relationship between UK private sector investment and UK economic growth as shown in the data. [3 marks]
   (b) Are there any reasons to expect a relationship between private sector investment and economic growth? [6 marks]
3. (a) Explain why public sector investment may move in the opposite direction to private sector investment. [5 marks]
   (b) Do the data in the table support this different relationship? [2 marks]
4. Discuss two measures, other than a change in public sector investment, which a government could take to stimulate economic growth. [6 marks]

Chapter Seven

Economic growth and markets

'Advocates of the "new economy" believe that IT has transformed the economy, enabling a golden period of rapid economic growth that will bring rapidly rising standards of living.'
Patrick Foley, Group Economic Advisor, Lloyds Bank

Economic growth reflects the performance of individual markets. Certain key markets can, at any one time, play a crucial role in determining the economic performance of the country. In turn they are themselves influenced by the rate of economic growth. In this chapter the interrelationships between economic growth and five markets are examined.

The housing market
● How the housing market affects economic growth
A strong housing market is usually taken as an indicator of a healthy economy, although if house prices are rising too rapidly it may be a sign of the economy overheating.

Rising activity in the housing market and the resulting rise in house prices may promote economic growth in four main ways:

● When people move house they often purchase new curtains, carpets and sometimes white goods, for example refrigerators and washing machines, and brown goods, for example televisions and cabinets. This increase in consumer expenditure will raise aggregate demand and stimulate a rise in output.
● House prices often go up by more than the rate of inflation and hence their real value rises. They also often go up by more than the rate of interest, so whilst the real value of a house rises, the real cost of mortgage interest payments falls. A house is the main asset that most people own, and when houses rise in price people feel wealthier and this may encourage them to spend more – there is a feel-good factor.
● Higher house prices may also enable people to borrow more easily by using their houses as security and, again because of increased confidence, may make them more willing to borrow.
● As well as increasing aggregate demand, a healthy housing market can raise the geographical mobility of labour. If it is relatively easy to

sell or rent houses people will find it easier to move from one part of the country to another. This will make it easier for firms wishing to expand to recruit labour and for firms wanting to contract to shed labour. As a result it becomes possible to use resources more fully and more efficiently – the economy's output point will move closer to the production possibility curve.

● How economic growth affects the housing market

Increases in GDP usually increase activity in the housing market. Housing has both positive income elasticity of demand and **income-elastic demand**. A rise in incomes enables new buyers to enter the market, some of those in the rented sector to move into the owner-occupied sector, and existing home owners to extend their properties or trade up. A buoyant economy also increases confidence and this encourages people to undertake greater financial commitments.

The UK has a higher proportion of people in owner-occupied accommodation than most European countries. For example, whereas 67 per cent of dwellings were owner-occupied in the UK in 1996, in France it was 54 per cent. In the UK, when incomes rise usually at least some of those in the rented sector will seek to move into owner-occupied accommodation.

Figure 20 shows that in the UK as the economy grew from 1961 to

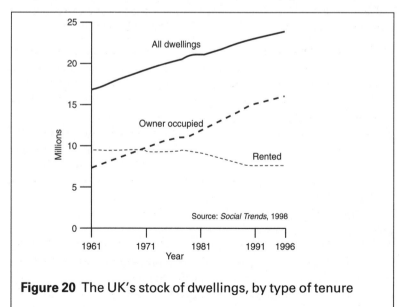

Figure 20 The UK's stock of dwellings, by type of tenure

1996 the number of owner-occupied dwellings more than doubled, whilst the number of rented dwellings fell by a sixth.

A slowdown in the growth of GDP or a fall in GDP has an adverse effect on the housing market. People become more reluctant to participate in the market. It becomes more difficult to sell houses and to rent out property. The price of housing may even fall. Some people may not be able to keep up with their mortgage payments and so may have their houses repossessed. Others may experience **negative equity**. This occurs when the market price of a property falls below the amount owed on the mortgage used to purchase it. Those people affected in this way will have great difficulty moving into other property.

The health market
● How the health market affects economic growth

Low levels of healthcare can hold back economic growth. In poor countries with low standards of healthcare, infant mortality, sickness and mortality rates are high.

However, in most developed countries healthcare expenditure makes a significant contribution to aggregate demand. A rise in spending on healthcare, whether it be private or public sector spending, will raise aggregate demand and is likely to increase the numbers employed in the industry. Healthcare is labour-intensive and employs large numbers of workers in many developed countries.

If higher spending on healthcare also results in a rise in the standard of care it will also increase the quality of the labour force. Fewer days will be lost through illness and absenteeism, and workers will produce higher and better quality output owing to their improved physical and mental condition.

● How economic growth affects the health market

Depending on how it is achieved, economic growth may increase or reduce mental and physical illness. If economic growth is accompanied by too rapid change and an increase in working hours, the mental and physical wellbeing of those in employment and those who lose their jobs may suffer. However, if it is achieved at a steady pace that people feel comfortable with, and its benefits are spread widely, the increased prosperity may increase the wellbeing of the population.

Nevertheless, however it is achieved economic growth is likely to result in increased demand for, and expenditure on, healthcare. Indeed there is usually a close correlation between GDP and health expenditure. Richer countries can afford to spend more on healthcare and usually do so. Demand rises because higher GDP and the resulting rise in material living standards enables people to live longer (and it is the elderly who place most demand on healthcare) and because demand for healthcare is income-elastic.

When incomes rise people also demand an improved quality of healthcare and are more likely to consult doctors and other medical staff at a lower pain threshold. As an economy grows, technology – including medical technology – is likely to advance. This makes possible not only more operations but also more expensive operations and operations which require expensive aftercare and medication.

One of the problems that countries experience as they grow is that demand for medical care tends to outstrip supply. Figure 21 illustrates demand for healthcare increasing by more than supply, which at any point in time tends to be fixed. In the diagram, there is an initial shortage of free healthcare equal to AQ; after a change in supply and demand the shortage is seen changing to BQ_1.

If healthcare is provided by the private sector this will result in a rise in price, and if it is provided by the public sector there will be a rise in waiting lists.

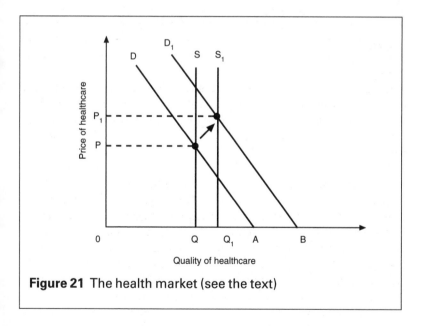

Figure 21 The health market (see the text)

The education market
● How education affects economic growth
Increased expenditure on education will raise aggregate demand and

increase the numbers employed in the industry, which in many countries is large. If this results in improved educational standards it will also raise the productivity of the workforce and thereby shift the long-run supply curve and the production possibility curve to the right.

The provision of more education can have different short-run and long-run effects. For example, an increase in a country's school leaving age will reduce the size of the working population and hence the workforce. In the short run this may reduce output. However, in the long run the rise in quality of the workforce is likely to more than offset the fall in the quantity of the workforce. So output is likely to increase. A rise in the proportion of school leavers going on to higher education is likely to have a similar effect.

An increase in the provision of nursery education may raise the size of the workforce in the short run and may increase the quality of the workforce in the longer run. Having more nursery school places should enable more parents, usually mothers, to re-enter the workforce. If the nursery education is of a good and appropriate standard it should

A little learning

Economists take two contrasting views on higher education. On the one hand, they regard higher education as a sort of intellectual sieve, designed merely to identify the brightest future employees, rather than to equip them with productive skills. On the other hand, economists regard education as an investment which builds 'human capital', making individuals more productive and thus benefiting society as a whole.

The sieving theory clearly makes some sense. Job advertisements specify 'graduate wanted'; companies trawl campuses to recruit future executives; many countries have rigid academic requirements for particular professions. All this helps to explain two striking facts: everywhere, graduates earn more than non-graduates; and everywhere, they are much less likely to be unemployed. ...

Society also benefits from those higher earnings, which result in higher tax revenues and lower payments for unemployment benefits and income support. But the gains are much smaller than those to individual students.

What else could justify society's investing in higher education? The common answer is that society as a whole also earns benefits in the form of faster economic growth. Recent economic research has supported the existence of a link by emphasizing the role of human capital in promoting growth and innovation. Societies which invest more in education, the argument goes, reap long-term rewards.

Plenty of evidence suggests that economies which invest little in education generally perform poorly.

The Economist, 13 December 1997

improve the educational performance of the children and their productivity when they enter the workforce.

● How economic growth affects education

As with healthcare, in some developing countries, low incomes mean that relatively few resources can be devoted to education. This contributes to the vicious circle of poverty – with low levels of education contributing to low productivity which in turn results in low incomes.

In contrast in developed countries there is usually a virtuous circle with high incomes enabling high expenditure on education which results in high productivity and hence high incomes.

As incomes rise demand for education increases. Again as with healthcare, demand for education is very income-elastic. Children stay on longer at school, more go on to higher education and more adults undertake leisure, academic and vocational courses. Table 8 shows the rise in those going into higher education in the UK.

Table 8 UK enrolments in higher education (males/females; thousands)

	1970/71	1980/81	1990/91	1995/96
Undergraduate				
Full-time	241/173	277/196	345/319	519/529
Part-time	127/19	176/71	193/148	221/310
Postgraduate				
Full-time	33/10	41/21	50/34	76/60
Part-time	15/3	32/13	50/36	98/89
All higher education	416/205	526/301	638/537	913/987

Source: ONS, *Social Trends* 28, 1998

Education provides both **investment and consumption benefits**. Undertaking education will raise peoples' skills and qualifications and thereby raise their earning potential (see the article from *The Times*). People may also enjoy the educational experience and it may generate interests which stay with them for life, such as reading, visiting the theatre and natural history.

Career-minded students think suits and anoraks

Hannah Betts

Statistics for 1999 show that degree course applicants are aiming at courses that will give them the best opportunities for gaining work.

Applications by March 24 show business and management studies consolidating its ranking as the most popular subject choice, with more than 120,000 applications. Computer science, with 80,000, is second favourite but shows the largest increase – 20 per cent – in popularity.

English, biology and sociology – subjects traditionally popular with sixth-formers – show falls ranging from 3.5 to 9 per cent. General and combined studies are down by 13 per cent.

These figures reflect a growing awareness that graduates with degrees which are vocational or numeracy-orientated are significantly more likely to be successful in finding appropriate work. According to a new report from the Institute for Employment Research of the University of Warwick, engineering and technology, business studies or maths and computing are all associated with career success.

At the same time, those with degrees in the arts and humanities, social sciences or natural sciences found their initial job-searching considerably less easy. Graduates with inter-disciplinary degrees are also suffering in the employment stakes.

The Times, 23 April 1999

The tourism market

● How tourism affects economic growth

In a number of countries tourism makes a major contribution to GDP and to increases in GDP. Indeed tourism is one of the most rapidly growing tertiary industries throughout the world. For example, tourism accounts for a quarter of the EU's exports of services. In many developing countries the figure is significantly higher.

Tourism brings in foreign revenue, creates employment and raise demand. Economists refer to the **tourism income multiplier**, which is the eventual change in income divided by the initial change in tourism expenditure. For instance, if tourism expenditure increases by £500 million and this results in GDP rising by £1500 million, the tourism income multiplier is three.

For many countries tourism is an important source of earnings in the trade-in-services section of their balance of payments. However, while some countries have a net surplus on tourism, others have a net deficit.

Tourism creates jobs directly in the tourist industry and indirectly via the tourism income multipler effect. Jobs in the tourism industry cover a range of activities, although a relatively high proportion are unskilled.

Tourism highlights the problem of achieving sustainable growth. If countries expand their tourist industry rapidly there may initially be high economic growth. However, the danger is that the rapid expansion may be achieved at high costs and in a manner which means that the growth cannot continue. For example, in developing countries, resources such as water may be diverted from use by the indigenous population (e.g. for irrigation) to be used by tourists in swimming pools. The existence of luxurious living conditions for tourists may cause some resentment among the inhabitants of poor countries.

The benefits of tourism may also not spread out into the wider population if the tourist complexes are largely self-contained and foreign-owned. For example, US tourists in India may not venture out of their US-owned holiday complexes, may eat mainly food imported from the US, watch US films and be entertained by US acts hired to appear at the holiday complexes.

There is also the risk that too rapid and unplanned expansion of the tourist industry may cause the destruction of the features of the area which appealed to the tourists in the first place. Bringing in too many tourists to an area of natural beauty may damage the natural environment and quiet atmosphere which they were seeking. For example, the natural environment in parts of Spain has been adversely affected by the erection of hotels along coastlines. The building of 'British' pubs, bingo halls and fish and chip shops has altered the atmosphere of some Spanish tourist resorts – in effect turning them into Spanish 'Blackpools'. Tourist centres have to consider very carefully what most of their consumers want and will want in the future.

People living in some parts of the UK resent the disruption caused to their lives by the high number of tourists who visit their regions in the peak periods. They dislike the congestion and the feeling that they are living in some type of theme park. The problem is made worse by the fact that tourism is not evenly spread in the UK. It is concentrated in a few areas.

To ensure that tourism can continue at the same or a higher rate, planners have to consider the **carrying capacity** of their tourist areas. In its widest sense, carrying capacity means the ability of an area to sustain a population at a given level of subsistence. It is often expressed as the maximum number of people per unit of land. It may also be defined more narrowly in the context of tourism to mean the maximum number of tourists an area can cope with in a way which does not

LAND AND FREEDOM

- Tourism is the world's largest growth industry – outstripping even the oil and the arms trades. In 1996, new records were set for international tourism: 592 million people travelled to destinations worldwide. ... Revenue from tourism amounted to $423 billion.

- Traditions are often a casualty of tourism. The Hula dance in Hawaii was once a solemn religious dance; its meaning has now been diluted so much that it is little more than a tourist sideshow. In Australia, thousands of tourists climb Ayers Rock – a practice that is deeply offensive to the aboriginal people as they consider the rock to be a sacred place.

- Tourism creates social change. Thirty-five years ago the mediterranean Spanish coast was a series of sleepy fishing villages. Today, almost the entire coastline from Barcelona to Gibraltar has been turned into one long resort. Along with the flood of visitors has come the high-rise hotels, clubs, bars, restaurants, traffic and the breakdown of long-standing family relationships. ... During the summer months there is a lot of work available, but at the end of the season many of the shops and restaurants close and the local residents are frequently left with no means of employment.

- Not all tourism is environmentally damaging; some sites have been reclaimed and restored thanks to outside interest, but there are many more that have been damaged by their popularity. The coral reefs off Kenya's coast have been ravaged by souvenir hunters looking to take a bit of the authentic African experience home with them. This not only endangers species dependent on the coral but can also increase the risk of shore erosion.

- Tourism creates jobs but it may also displace other forms of livelihood. Moreover, the financial benefits are frequently not passed on into the local economy. The Gambia has established itself as a relatively low-budget holiday destination offering all-inclusive deals where guests need never leave the confines of their hotel. Local inhabitants may be able to pick up low-paid catering or cleaning work, but there are few, if any, opportunities for the community as a whole to benefit. Even food producers are side-lined as hotels tend to import most of their food so that they can offer a standardized western menu that will be immediately familiar to their guests.

- Tourism is a notoriously fickle industry. Resorts and hotels can easily go out of favour with the public; if this happens after a community has diverted all its economic activity into leisure, the consequences can be devastating.

Source: Extracts from 'Land and freedom' by John Crace, *The Guardian* (Education Section), 4 May 1999

damage the features that attract the tourists. These include the environment, the culture and the facilities of the area.

- ● How economic growth affects tourism

Tourism is very income-elastic. As incomes rise, demand for holidays increases, usually by a greater percentage. This includes holidays both at home and abroad, although it is foreign tourism which is the most income-elastic.

As a country's GDP rises its people are able to afford to go on more holidays and to go on more expensive ones. They may also have more time to be on holiday. People in developed countries usually work fewer hours and fewer weeks than those in developing countries.

As a country develops, some of the facilities initially created for foreign tourists become affordable to the country's own people.

The information technology market
- ● How the IT industry affects economic growth

In many countries IT is the fastest-growing industry. It accounts for a significant number of new jobs created in the USA, Europe and the Far East (see the boxed item).

It creates new products and puts downward pressure on inflation over time as IT products, and products made using advanced IT, fall in price. Investment in IT also increases the productivity of the industries which use it. Its application in education raises the productivity of future workers. So it causes the current and future LRAS and production possibility curves to shift to the right.

The IT industry is an important engine for economic growth as it is one that can reap significant economies of scale. For example, whilst it was relatively expensive to develop and produce the first compact disk (CD) thereafter the marginal costs incurred in producing extra units was low. As well as supply-side economies of scale, the IT industry enjoys **demand-side economies of scale**. The more consumers there are, the greater the advantages to each consumer. For example, a consumer of an e-mail facility will benefit the more people have e-mail addresses.

However, the application of IT also illustrates the risk of rapid change which can be associated with economic growth. The introduction of IT in the workplace, in shops and in the home has changed the pattern of work and home life. Some people find this easier to cope with than others. Those who are not IT literate find it more difficult to gain and retain employment and do not have access to the range of information, purchasing opportunities and activities which those who are IT literate have. However, IT is becoming increasingly user-friendly.

The importance of the IT industry

IT investment now accounts for nearly 50 per cent of US businesses' capital spending, compared with 30 per cent ten years ago and less than 10 per cent twenty years ago. The share of computing and communications in the US gross domestic product has risen from 4.5 per cent in 1980 to an estimated 8.5 per cent in 1998. And this sector's contribution to US economic growth has been out of proportion to its share of GDP: in recent years the IT sector has accounted for more than one-quarter of US economic growth.

In the five years to 1997, average annual growth in the UK computer services market was 12 per cent; in 1997 growth is estimated at 14 per cent. More than a million people work in the UK's computer services industry, 300,000 of them in jobs created since 1993. This figure includes people working at user companies and for external suppliers. Growth among suppliers has been strongest, with a rise of 20 per cent, or 60,000 jobs in the past year. The UK industry is growing faster than in other European countries. It is estimated that 10 per cent of all new jobs created over the last 5 years are in IT services.

It is widely believed that investment in information and communication technology has had wider beneficial effects on output growth in recent years, allowing, for instance, the US economy to reach employment recently that in the past would have been associated with rapidly rising inflation.

Most striking of all aspects of IT's expanding role in the economy has been the recent explosive growth of the Internet. The Internet has been described rightly as the fastest-growing consumer market ever. Between 1989 and 1995, Internet use roughly doubled every year. Since 1995 growth has been even faster. According to the Computer Industry Almanac, there were 100 million Internet users worldwide by the end of last year, with 55 million of these in the USA and 22 million in Europe. By end-2000, the Almanac predicts 327 million users worldwide, of which 132 million will be in the USA and 102 million in Europe. In the UK, the number of users is expected to rise from 5.8 to 17 million in the same three-year period.

Source: 'A new (micro) economy' by Patrick Foley, *Lloyds Bank Economic Bulletin*, December 1998

- How economic growth affects IT

Economic growth will result in an expansion of the IT industry for a number of reasons:

- *Increased purchasing power.* As with the products of the other markets examined in this chapter, IT has an income-elastic demand. The most affluent tend to be the first users of new IT.
- *Increased optimism.* This is likely to make firms want to expand and so they increase their demand for IT products.
- *Education.* Countries with high GDP are likely to devote more resources, including IT resources, to education.
- *Healthcare.* Demand for and the output of healthcare is likely to rise and the healthcare industry is a major user of IT products.

KEY WORDS

Income-elastic demand
Negative equity
Investment and consumption
   benefits

Tourism income multiplier
Carrying capacity
Demand-side economies of
   scale

Further reading

Atkinson, B., Livesey, F. and Milward, R., Chapters 10, 12 and 16 in *Applied Economics*, Macmillan, 1998.

Cooper, C. *et al.*, Chapter 1 in *Tourism, Principles and Practice*, Addison-Wesley Longman, 1998.

Griffiths, A. and Wall, S. (eds), Chapter 12 in *Applied Economics*, 7th edn, Addison-Wesley Longman, 1997.

Maunder, P., Myers, D., Wall, N. and Miller, R., Chapter 11 in *Economics Explained*, 3rd edn, Collins Educational, 1995.

Useful websites

BIZ/ed: www.bized.ac.uk/
The Guardian: www.guardian.co.uk/

Essay topics

1. (a) Explain why education and healthcare are regarded as merit goods. [10 marks]

   (b) Discuss the contributions that education and healthcare can make to economic growth. [15 marks]

2. Assess the advantages and disadvantages that a developing country may experience as a result of expanding its tourist industry. [25 marks]

Data response question

This task is based on a question set by the University of London Examinations and Assessment Council in 1998. Read the piece below, which is adapted from 'Tourism: a major contribution to Britain' by A. Bliss, published in *Public Policy Review* in 1994. Then answer the questions that follow.

Tourism in the UK

By the year 2000 tourism will be the world's biggest industry. Estimates by the World Tourism and Travel Council put the annual value of trade in world tourism at over $2.5 trillion (thousand billion) dollars – a staggering 5.5 per cent of world GDP. Receipts from international tourism (about 20 per cent of all tourism expenditure) have expanded at an average annual growth rate of over 13 per cent between 1970 and 1992. The UK has been a major beneficiary of this massive growth in international tourism. Our share of world arrivals in 1992 was 3.9 per cent and we captured 5 per cent of all international tourism receipts.

In the ten years to 1992, UK tourism recorded better foreign exchange earnings growth than all other leading export sectors apart from transport and electrical equipment manufacturers. Tourism's share of gross domestic product in 1992 was 3.4 per cent (excluding day-visitor spending) and tourism-related purchases accounted for around 5.3 per cent of all consumer spending in Britain. Transport, petroleum, retail and other industries benefit from purchases directly allied to tourism. Tourism stimulates further, indirect spending elsewhere in the economy, equivalent to an estimated 50–70 per cent of direct tourism-related expenditure.

There are well over 220,000 tourism-related businesses in Britain employing almost 1.5 million people – around 6 per cent of the entire workforce – and embracing a further 183,000 self-employed jobs.

On the other hand, the large number of tourists visiting London causes considerable external costs for those who live and work in the capital.

It is inevitable that the British will wish to experience the cultures and climates of other countries. As a result, expenditure by UK residents on holidays abroad increased by 40 per cent in the 1980s, while expenditure on holidays at home declined. Many of the factors influencing travel decisions, such as exchange rates, are out of our control.

1. What do the data on trade in world tourism imply about the income elasticity of demand for travel? [2 marks]
2. Explain the multiplier effects of tourism on the UK economy. [6 marks]
3. What arguments could you use in support of the case for the UK government promoting the tourism industry in the UK? [4 marks]
4. It has been argued that the growth of tourism has an adverse effect of the local environment.
   (a) Identify *two* examples of external costs arising from an increase in the number of foreign tourists visiting London. [2 marks]
   (b) Suggest how the UK government could tackle these problems. [5 marks]
5. Analyse *three* factors that affect the demand for travel abroad by UK residents. [6 marks]

Chapter Eight

The nature and causes of business cycles

> '*The modern world regards business cycles much as the ancient Egyptians regarded the overflowing of the Nile. The phenomenon recurs at intervals; it is of great importance to everyone, and natural causes of it are not in sight.*'
> *John Clark*

Definition

Business or trade cycles are fluctuations in economic activity; moving from periods of boom to recession and back again. As a result they are also sometimes called *boom–bust cycles*. What is fluctuating is actual economic growth. Whilst potential economic growth tends to rise relatively steadily, actual economic growth can vary around this long-run trend, sometimes quite significantly.

Figure 22 shows the UK business cycle from 1961 to 1997. Contractions in economic activity occurred in, for example, the early 1980s and early 1990s.

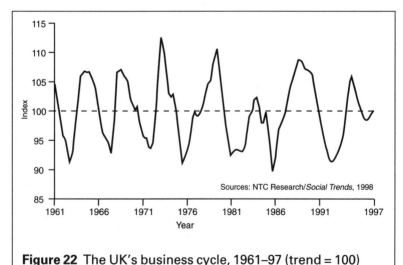

Figure 22 The UK's business cycle, 1961–97 (trend = 100)

The existence of the business cycle

For a period of time in the 1960s it was suggested by some economists that the business cycle was dead. Even more recently in the late 1990s some economists have argued that, owing to global competition and technological advances, developed countries would experience steady economic growth and low inflation. However, most economists believe that business cycles remain a real risk. This belief has been reinforced by the recent global crisis.

Phases of the business cycle

Economists usually identify four key phases of the business cycle (see Figure 23).

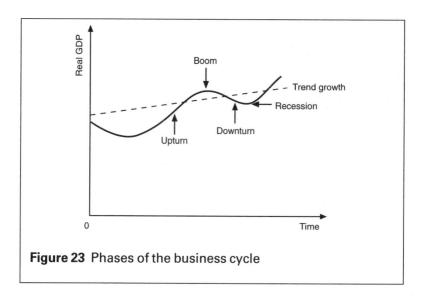

Figure 23 Phases of the business cycle

● Upturn

Upturn can also be referred to as the upswing or recovery. During this phase the economy is expanding. Output, income and aggregate demand increase. This makes consumers and entrepreneurs become more optimistic, which in turn further stimulates aggregate demand. Profits rise and banks expand credit. Entrepreneurs increase investment and employment. This is the phase when the rate of economic growth is likely to be at its highest. The economy will be performing well although there may be early signs of inflationary pressures.

● Boom

The **boom** can also be called the peak. This is the top of the business cycle. The gap between actual and potential output narrows and the level of output is at its highest point. Investment, employment and income are, as a consequence, also high.

However, as aggregate demand continues to increase and eventually exceeds the productive capacity of the economy, problems begin to be encountered. The economy becomes **supply-constrained**. Resources become scarcer and it becomes increasingly difficult for aggregate supply to keep pace with aggregate demand. For example, shortages of skilled workers will develop. The more rapid growth in aggregate demand results in inflation and balance of payments difficulties.

These problems are reinforced by the fact that, during this phase, with high levels of profit and credit, individuals increase their borrowing to high levels and firms undertake risky investments. Projects and new businesses which would not normally be regarded as viable are set up and less efficient factors of production are employed.

● Downturn

In the **downturn** the rate of economic growth starts to slow. There will have been a loss of price competitiveness. Output and incomes rise more slowly. Entrepreneurs and consumers become less optimistic. Firms postpone or cancel some of their investment projects and reduce their orders for raw materials and components. Consumers become concerned about the possibility of rising unemployment and so start to build up their savings.

The resulting fall in the growth of aggregate demand causes the rate of actual growth to fall below the trend rate.

● Recession

A **recession** can also be referred to as a trough and is a period of negative growth (i.e. falling GDP) over a period of at least two quarters.

During this phase confidence and aggregate demand fall. Investment expenditure is cut and unemployment rises. Inefficient firms go out of business. Through the multiplier and accelerator effects this causes a further fall in aggregate demand and economic activity. There may be negative net investment with firms not replacing worn-out machines. The economy may experience a **depression** (slump) with declining output and a high level of unemployment existing over a long period.

However, the downturn will sooner or later run its course. It will be **demand-constrained** as consumption and investment cannot fall to zero. Consumers eventually have to replace, say, old furniture and cars, and eventually firms will have to replace at least some worn-out capital equipment and stocks.

Types of business cycle
Economists identify a variety of business cycles, distinguished by their causes and duration.

● Kitchin cycles
Kitchin cycles – named after Joseph Kitchin who discussed them in an article published in 1923 – are thought to be caused by industry increasing and reducing inventories (i.e. stocks). It is claimed that they last between three and five years.

● Juglar cycles
Juglar cycles – named after a French economist Clement Juglar (1819–1905) – are also called *investment cycles* and are associated with changes in net investment. Juglar identified the key indicators of business cycles to be changes in prices, interest rates, borrowing and the money supply. It is thought that Juglar cycles last for approximately 8–10 years.

● Kuznets cycles
Kuznets cycles – named after a Russian economist Simon Kuznets (1901–85) – are also known as *building cycles*. They are connected with changes in activity in the construction and associated industries. Kuznets studied the US economy in particular (where he worked) and suggested that these changes in construction could be caused by large-scale immigration. The average duration given for these cycles is 16–20 years.

● Kondratieff cycles
Kondratieff cycles – named after a Russian economist Nikolai Kondratieff (1892–1931) – are the longest cycle described, of 50–60 years. Kondratieff claimed that there are long as well as short business cycles. He concentrated on describing rather than explaining the long-run fluctuations in economic activity ('long waves') he believed existed. He argued that prices move with the cycle, rising in the upswing and falling in the downswing. Although he did not provide a definite explanation for the cycles, he suggested that they could be the result of shocks to the system such as wars and discoveries of gold.

Joseph Schumpeter, the influential Austrian economist, explained the

Juglar and Kondratieff cycles by changes in the level of innovations, with **innovations** starting to **cluster** during a downturn and being applied on a large scale during an upturn.

A cycle far from dead

Samuel Brittan

The trendy slogan is that the business cycle is dead. Even as solid a journal as *Foreign Affairs* runs in its July issue an article by Steven Weber, an associate professor of political science, who maintains that the waves of the business cycle are becoming ripples. He argues that 'smarter government policy, globalization, changes in technology and emerging markets, all cushion shocks and dampen the familiar boom and bust'.

In the same issue of that journal (which is rapidly becoming the leading forum for such debates) the economist Professor Paul Krugman assures us that the business cycle is alive and kicking.

The economy oscillates in response to shocks which can come in various forms, including Japanese financial bubbles, Middle Eastern wars and German unification. Prof. Krugman goes on to explain that, for these shocks to produce recessions, two things must be in place.

First, there has to be a system of paper credit, which sooner or later contracts. Second, a substantial proportion of the economy must respond to drops in demand by cutting production rather than prices. Otherwise the financial contraction will only lead to price deflation without a fall in output. Of course Prof. Krugman is right – and it is worth remembering that pronouncements about 'the end of the business cycle' were just as prevalent when the long US recovery of the late 1960s was running its course as they are now.

Financial Times, 28 August 1997

Explanations of business cycles

A range of explanations are advanced for business cycles. Some are essentially *endogenous*, concentrating on events occurring within the economy. Others are *exogenous*, being based on events occurring outside the particular economy. Below a few of the explanations are discussed.

● The Keynesian explanation

The main Keynesian explanation is an endogenous one based on the inter-reaction of the multiplier and accelerator effects. This view emphasizes the cumulative nature of business cycles.

It is argued that an injection of extra spending, perhaps in the form of an increase in government spending, will cause GDP to rise by a multiple amount. As it increases, investment rises by a greater percentage (the accelerator theory) thereby increasing the rate of growth. However, when the full-capacity level is reached, investment opportunities will decline and the marginal efficiency of capital (the rate of return on investment) may fall. Problems of shortages, inflation and balance of payments deficit will occur and the rate of growth of GDP will start to decline. The growth of output may start to decline even before the full-capacity level is reached, if the government, fearing that the economy may overheat, tightens fiscal and monetary policy.

Whatever the cause, when the slowdown occurs investment will fall, again by a greater percentage, and this time this will cause a multiple decline in GDP. The fall in GDP in turn reduces investment. This downward spiral continues until a floor of minimum consumption and investment is reached or government action is taken.

● Innovation clusters

This is another endogenous explanation which has had some famous exponents. Kondratieff and Schumpeter (see above) in their work on long waves argued that diffusion of new technology takes time but has significant effects.

Recent studies, particularly by G. Mensch, have built on this work . He suggests that economic growth is characterized by spurts of innovation. He believes that when there is a high and increasing level of economic activity there is little incentive to innovate. Firms introduce only minor changes to their methods of production and the range of products. Their spending on research and development may not rise. However, when economic activity is declining and profits are falling, firms come under more pressure to adopt new technologies. This creates new products, new industries and increases aggregate demand. This tendency for innovation to be concentrated into particular periods results in fluctuations in economic activity.

● Political cycles

Political cycles can occur as a result of changes in the priority given to different macroeconomic objectives and the timing of general elections.

A government's initial priority may be economic growth and so it adopts measures to stimulate growth. However, if inflation and balance-of-payments difficulties arise a government may switch its priorities. The policies it now adopts – for example, higher taxation – are likely to slow down the growth rate (stop–go policies).

As a government approaches a general election it may seek to stimulate economic activity. Just after an election has been won, more unpopular, deflationary policy measures may be adopted if inflation and balance of payments problems exist.

● **Fluctuations in the money supply**

Monetarists argue that fluctuations in economic activity can occur as result of the government increasing the money supply at a rate in excess of the increase in output. This initially stimulates economic activity and the growth rate increases. However, in the longer run the higher demand will create inflation. This will reduce the country's price competitiveness and hence demand for its goods and services both at home and abroad.

● **Shocks**

Shocks are unexpected events which throw an economy's growth pattern off course. They can come in the form of *demand-side or supply-side shocks*. For example, the decline in demand for European and American goods from Asian countries which occurred in the late 1990s was not widely predicted even a couple of years beforehand.

In 1998 El Niño related phemonena created a supply-side shock in many parts of Africa, Asia and Latin America. Countries' actual and potential growth were harmed by both storms and by drought. Crops, water supplies and rural infrastructure were all destroyed.

KEY WORDS

Upturn	Kitchin cycles
Boom	Juglar cycles
Supply-constrained	Kuznets cycles
Downturn	Kondratieff cycles
Recession	Innovation clusters
Depression	Political cycles
Demand-constrained	Shocks

Further reading

Anderton, A., Unit 67 in *Economics*, 2nd edn, Causeway Press, 1995.

Grant, S., Chapter 56 in *Stanlake's Introductory Economics*, 7th edn, Addison-Wesley Longman, 1999.

Smith, D., Chapter 6 in *UK Current Economic Policy*, 2nd edn, Heinemann Educational, 1999.

Solomou, S., *Economic Cycles*, Manchester University Press, 1998.

Useful websites
Daily Telegraph: www.telegraph.co.uk/
The Times: www.the-times.co.uk/

Essay topics
1. (a) What are the main characteristics of a recession? [10 marks]
   (b) Analyse the cause of fluctuations in economic activity. [15 marks]
2. (a) Explain how the multiplier effect takes place. [6 marks]
   (b) The 1990s saw reductions in direct tax rates together with an increased marginal propensity to import. Explain the way in which these changes have affected the size of the multiplier. [12 marks]
   (c) Assess the advantages and disadvantages of increases in government expenditure, compared with reductions in income tax rates as methods of raising GDP. [22 marks] [University of Oxford Delegacy of Local Examinations 1998]

Data response question
This task is based on a question set by the University of Cambridge Local Examinations Syndicate in 1996. Read the article below (by D. Wong), which appeared in *Straits Times* on 13 November 1993. Then answer the questions that follow.

Economy posts 9.2 per cent growth in third quarter

The Singapore economy grew by 9.2 per cent in the third quarter of this year [1993]. As growth remained broad-based, and the electronics industry and stock market are expected to continue their good performance, the government has raised its growth forecast for the whole year to about 9 per cent.

This is an improvement on its projection of 7.5–8 per cent annual growth made in August, which was itself a revision from an earlier forecast of 6–7 per cent.

The Ministry of Trade and Industry, however, expects economic growth to ease next year, and has made a tentative forecast of 6–8 per cent growth for 1994.

A spokesman noted that the electronics industry was cautious and the construction sector was slowing down because of fewer contracts this year.

The manufacturing sector continued its strong and rapid growth, in particular the electronics and petroleum industries. Overall, the sector grew by 10.9 per cent. 'Overall growth was fuelled by both external and

Vital signs

	1st quarter	2nd quarter	3rd quarter
Economic growth	7.3%	10.4%	9.2%
No. of jobs created	16,300	12,500	19,100
Inflation	2.4%	2.3%	2.4%
Productivity	4.9%	7.5%	5.2%*

* Singapore's products are still competitive in international markets because productivity has kept pace with wage increases.

How the sectors performed

Financial services
17.6%
Stock market boost moderated by slower bank lending

Construction
8.4%
Construction contracts totalled $2.3 billion

Manufacturing
10.9%
Biggest growth: electronics, petroleum industries

Commerce
8.2%
Growth leader: robust entrepot trade

Transport and communication
9.1%
Cargo and passenger traffic slowed

Business services
3.9%
Generally upbeat except for fall in real estates sector

domestic demand, and productivity growth is now at a sustainable 5.2 per cent,' said the spokesman.

Industrialists and businessmen are moderately optimistic about the business prospects according to the ministry's survey of business expectations for the fourth quarter. 'Businessmen are still concerned about the stagnated growth of the developed countries and growth will probably have to come again from the ASEAN [Association of Southeast Asian Nations] countries and southern China,' said the spokesman.

1. (a) Describe Singapore's growth record in the first three quarters of 1993. [1 mark]

   (b) How did the government's latest overall growth forecast of 1993 (see the article) compare with earlier estimates? [2 marks]

   (c) Why was this latest forecast likely to be the more accurate? [2 marks]

2. What can be deduced from the article about Singapore's economic relationship with the rest of the world in 1993? [3 marks]

3. (a) What was the relationship between changes in productivity growth and economic growth in Singapore? [1 mark]

   (b) According to the information, Singapore's productivity kept pace with wage increases. Explain the economic significance of this. [2 marks]

   (c) Consider the problems of any one method of raising productivity. [3 marks]

4. Evaluate the likely effects of a fast rate of economic growth in an economy [6 marks]

Chapter Nine

The global financial crisis

'The Western world is experiencing its most serious crisis in fifty years.'
Alan Greenspan, Chairman of the American Reserve

The quote manages to capture some of the concern being expressed throughout the world about the **global financial crisis** which originated in East Asia. This major event showed how difficult it is for countries to sustain steady economic growth, the forces which can operate to turn a high level of economic growth into a downswing, and how a country's growth rate can be threatened by events in other countries.

The background

The difficulties really began in mid 1997 among East Asian economies which had previously enjoyed high economic growth.

Thailand was the first country to experience problems. Its firms had borrowed heavily. The economy overheated. Its earnings from exports fell and some firms got into financial difficulties. The Thai government stated it would not help out struggling companies. Some did go out of business, being unable to repay their debts.

Thailand, as with the other East Asian 'tigers', had previously attracted a considerable amount of overseas financial and capital investment. The defaulting on debt led to a loss of confidence and an outflow of capital. The country was forced to devalue its currency and then had to secure a loan from the International Monetary Fund (IMF).

The next country to be affected was South Korea. Firms in South Korea had also borrowed heavily and were badly hit by falling prices for computer memory chips, cars and steel. Again capital flowed out of the country. The problems then spread to Malaysia, Indonesia, the Philippines and Japan. They were exacerbated by speculators seeking to gain from the large changes in exchange rates and share prices.

When the Japanese economy experienced trouble, the west really became concerned. Japan went into recession, with output and the general price level falling and unemployment rising. The Japanese economy had been held up as a model, thriving economy. It also had considerable investments in both Europe and the USA.

The crisis then moved on to destabilize the economies of Russia and several Latin American economies, including Brazil, Argentina and Venezuela. The countries had to devalue their currencies, some of their banks collapsed, and they witnessed falls in share prices. They found it increasingly difficult and expensive to borrow as financial investors became more aware of the risks of defaulting on debt.

In 1998, the East Asian countries went into recession. For instance, South Korea's economic growth changed from 6.3 per cent in 1997 to *minus* 6.6 per cent in 1998. Indonesia experienced an even more dramatic change, from an 8.0 per cent growth rate in 1997 to a *minus* 16.5 per cent rate in 1998.

The deflationary effects began to be felt in Europe and the United States. Growth rates slowed and fears were expressed that the west would slip into recession.

The quote at the beginning of the chapter is taken from a speech that Alan Greenspan gave in October 1998 when he acknowledged the seriousness of the situation. The cartoon on the previous page (from the cover of *The Economist*) also shows Alan Greenspan and reflects his view of the threat facing the world and his determination to take action to reverse the deflationary effects.

Origins of the crisis

The origins of the crisis were similar in cause to those which, in the past, have resulted in downturns in the business cycle in a number of countries. However, this time the downturn was particularly severe and spread widely throughout the world.

When an economy is enjoying a boom, especially if that has lasted for some time, its banks and companies become over-confident. Banks are willing and anxious to lend. They often do not look too closely into the viability of the companies they lend to nor into the projects those companies wish to undertake. Indeed, during a boom firms and individuals take on excessive levels of debt, a number of inefficient firms may be able to survive and these, and other firms, may seek to borrow in order to undertake very risky projects.

This is what occurred in Thailand and the other East Asian countries. Its banks had lent, frequently with few questions asked , on speculative projects, especially in property and construction. The banks had, themselves, attracted funds from abroad. When the returns on the projects failed to live up to expectations the banks had difficulty repaying creditors and some banks collapsed. This reduced confidence and made foreign investors reluctant to place their money in East Asia.

There may have been an element of **moral hazard**. This occurs when individuals and/or companies take more risks than they would do in the absence of an insurance company or another body covering any possible losses. Some of the foreign investors in East Asia, Russia and Latin America may have believed that the governments of the countries would have bailed out companies in difficulties. As a result they may not have checked the creditworthiness of the companies and may have lent more than was appropriate. When companies started to default and their governments did not step in, the foreign investors reassessed their investment decisions and in some cases withdrew their funds.

It might also be claimed that the weaknesses revealed in the banking systems of the East Asian countries, and the reduction in economic drive which some economists claimed to have found among East Asian entrepreneurs, gives some credence to the convergence theory. As countries that had been doing well they had not questioned whether

Table 9 World growth, 1981–2007 (annual percentage change in real GDP*)

Region	1981–90	1991–97	1997	Forecasts 1998	1999	2000	2001–07	Previous year's forecast
World total	3.1	2.3	3.2	1.8	1.9	2.7	3.2	3.4
High-income countries	3.1	2.1	2.8	1.7	1.6	2.3	2.6	2.8
OECD countries	3.0	2.0	2.7	1.9	1.6	2.2	2.5	2.7
Non-OECD countries	6.6	6.4	5.3	-1.8	2.0	3.9	5.2	5.7
Developing countries	3.0	3.1	4.8	2.0	2.7	4.3	5.2	5.5
East Asia	7.7	9.9	7.1	1.3	4.8	5.9	6.6	7.5
Europe and Central Asia	2.6	-4.4	2.6	0.5	0.1	3.4	5.0	5.2
Latin America and the Caribbean	1.9	3.4	5.1	2.5	0.6	3.3	4.4	4.4
Middle East and North Africa	1.0	2.9	3.1	2.0	2.8	3.1	3.7	3.7
South Asia	5.7	5.7	5.0	4.6	4.9	5.6	5.5	5.9
Sub-Saharan Africa	1.9	2.2	3.5	2.4	3.2	3.8	4.1	4.2
Memorandum items								
East Asian crisis countries†	6.9	7.2	4.5	-8.0	0.1	3.2	5.2	6.8
Transition countries of Europe and Central Asia	2.4	-5.5	1.7	-0.4	-0.6	3.0	4.8	5.3
Developing countries, excluding the transition countries	3.3	5.3	5.3	2.5	3.2	4.5	5.2	5.6
Developing countries, excluding transition and ASEAN-4††	3.1	5.1	5.5	3.9	3.6	4.7	5.2	5.4

*GDP is measured at market prices and expressed in 1987 prices and exchange rates. Growth rates over historic intervals are computed using least-squares method.

† Indonesia, Republic of Korea, Malaysia, Philippines and Thailand.

†† Asian crisis countries, excluding Republic of Korea.

Source: World Bank data and baseline projections, November 1998

their institutions, in particular their financial institutions, were still appropriate for the demands of the late 1990s and had begun to take a high living standard for granted. Since the start of the crisis, of course, reforms have taken place to the financial systems throughout East Asia.

Table 9 shows the dramatic reversal of the fortunes of the 'East Asian crisis countries' in 1998 and the effect this had on the growth rates of other countries.

Why did the contagion spread so far?

With the globalization of goods, capital and financial markets, events in one region can quickly affect other countries. This spread can be referred to as a **systemic crisis** when it is serious enough to threaten the world economy. The '**Asian contagion**' spread via a number of factors (see also the article from *The Times*).

- The devaluations in the Far East had the effect of making imports from the East Asian countries more price-competitive and exports into East Asia less price-competitive. As a result demand for other countries' goods and services, both from East Asian customers and their own citizens, fell.
- Falling incomes in East Asia reduced the ability of people and companies in East Asia to demand goods and services from other countries, including commodities from Russia and Latin America. Indeed commodity prices fell significantly in 1998.
- East Asian companies based abroad (e.g. Japanese multinationals such as Fujitsu) cut back on staff and cancelled investment projects.
- There were reductions in business and consumer confidence throughout the world resulting from witnessing what had happened to previously prosperous economies.
- There was a reduction in investors being willing to lend to developing economies and economies making the transition from planned to market economies because of their having experienced a number of debt defaults, mostly notably those of Thailand and Russia.
- A **credit crunch** developed. Banks increased the gap between the interest rate at which they would lend and the rate they would pay their depositors. They also became more cautious in their lending policies and made their lending criteria more stringent. This reduced consumer demand and made it difficult for firms to borrow when they had cash-flow problems and when they wanted to invest. Some firms did go out of business. Figure 24 illustrates a credit crunch.

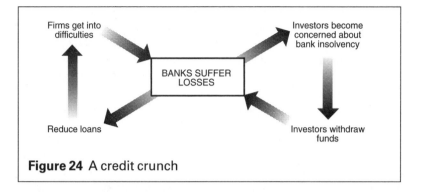

Figure 24 A credit crunch

Financial crashes share common cause

P. Durwen

The South Sea bubble burst in 1720. Financial crashes before and since have a common thread: they spring from the momentum of markets outstripping economic realities. The devastation of the financial system in 17th-century Amsterdam, the great Wall Street correction of October 1987, and the Thai collapse of 1997, which precipitated the current crisis in world markets, all have their roots in prices over-reaching values.

In America over the past year, share prices had risen far beyond the conventional ratings of previous booms. Investors theorized that a new age had dawned in which trade cycles had finally been brought under control. Faith in that paradigm is now ... shuddering.

Roughly a year passed between the collapse of the East Asian tiger economies, the cause of the current western crash, and the impact finally overcoming upward trends in western markets. The lag is not unusual. The most devastating crash is still that of Wall Street in 1929, which caused US share prices to lose nearly 90 per cent of their peak value by the nadir in 1932. But share prices had kept climbing as the US economy had started turning down into recession in the spring of 1929, and began to crash only in the summer.

Crashes cause an economic depression if, as in 1930s America or 1997 Korea, falling share prices cause a mass of financial failures, bad debts and a shrinkage of bank credit. Britain's worse bear market was in 1972–75, when share prices fell by two thirds in the wake of oil price rises, higher interest rates and a shortage of credit to finance inflation and did not regain their 1972 peak until late 1977. Asia's 1997 financial crash has probably inaugurated a decade of depression as severe as the 1930s were in the west. In the west today, however, share price falls may just be a natural reaction to slower world growth, not the cause of depression.

The Times, 7 October 1998

Measures taken to deal with the Asian contagion

As already mentioned, reforms were introduced to the banking systems in East Asia. Japan sought to boost aggregate demand to reverse the decline in its output. It introduced a number of measures, including reduced interest rates and taxes and raised government spending. However, it was having to combat the Japanese traditional high marginal propensity to save which, in the light of fears over unemployment, increased.

In the west, Alan Greenspan led the way by cutting US interest rates to boost confidence, stimulate aggregate demand and mitigate the effects of the credit crunch. Europe, including the UK, followed suit. The west and the IMF also offered financial support to the countries in trouble.

Fluctuations in economic activity

The global financial crisis has shown that even what had been perceived as strong countries can still fall into recession and indeed still run the risk of experiencing a depression. It has also demonstrated how interlinked the economies of the world are, how quickly and significantly they can be affected by events outside their own countries, and the need for concerted world action to restore and then maintain steady and sustainable economic growth.

KEY WORDS

Global financial crisis   Asian contagion
Moral hazard   Credit crunch
Systemic crisis

Further reading

Atkinson, B., Livesey, F. and Milward, R., Chapter 28 in *Applied Economics*, Macmillan, 1998.

Curwen, P., Chapter 2 in *Understanding the UK Economy*, 4th edn, Macmillan, 1997.

Grant, S., Chapter 56 in *Stanlake's Introductory Economics*, 7th edn, Longman, 1999.

Griffiths, A. and Wall, S., Chapter 27 in *Applied Economics*, 7th edn, Addison-Wesley Longman, 1997.

Useful websites
IMF: www.imf.org/
World Bank: www.worldbank.org/

Essay topics
1. Analyse the implications for output, employment and prices in the UK of a major recession in the United States. [20 marks] [University of Oxford Delegacy of Local Examinations 1996]
2. (a) Analyse the causes of the global financial crisis. [15 marks]
   (b) Discuss whether you think it could have been avoided. [10 marks]

Data response question
This task is based on a question set by the University of Cambridge Local Examinations Syndicate in 1996. Read the following information, taken from *A Planner's Guide to International Market Conditions* (Euromonitor, 1993). Then answer the questions that follow.

An economic profile of Japan

Japan has [in 1993] the world's second largest GDP after the USA, and enjoys a large trade surplus with the rest of the world. The Japanese government came under considerable international pressure in the late 1980s to reduce its trade surplus. It attempted to do this by reducing interest rates in order to boost domestic demand.

Despite its present strength, economic growth is expected to slow down. Furthermore, Japan's ageing population is likely to lead to increased government expenditure on pensions and healthcare provision in the future.

Tables A, B and C give some economic data.

Table A Japan: an economic profile

	1990	1991
GDP (% change calculated at constant prices)	5.2	4.5
GDP per capita (US$)	23 800	27 135
Consumer prices (% change)	3.1	3.3
Components of GDP (%)		
Government consumption	9.1	9.2
Private consumption	57.4	56.8
Gross fixed capital formation	32.2	31.6
Exchange rate (yen per US$)	144.79	134.71
Exports (US$ billion)	287.6	314.8
Imports (US$ billion)	235.4	237.0

Source: Euromonitor

Table B Major trading partners (percentage share in latest year)

	Exports	Imports
USA/Canada	36.5	27.4
Western Europe	20.5	15.9
EC [now EU]	17.5	13.4

Source: Euromonitor

Table C Japan's labour force and projected population change, 1990–2010

	1990	2010
Total population (millions)	123	133
Employed and self-employed (millions)	62	62
Activity rate (%)*	50.20	46.90

* Defined as the percentage of the total population which is economically active.
Source: ILO, Euromonitor

1. Japan attempted to reduce its trade surplus by lowering its interest rates.
   (a) Calculate Japan's trade surplus with the rest of the world in 1990. [1 mark]
   (b) Explain how a reduction in interest rates might help to reduce Japan's trade surplus. [3 marks]

(c) To what extent was the policy successful between 1990 and 1991? [3 marks]

(d) Consider how other changes shown in the data may have affected the success of the policy. [4 marks]

2. (a) Compare the change in the total population with the change in the economically active population. [1 mark]

(b) Identify *two* influences on the activity rate of an economy. [2 marks]

3. Japan's government expenditure on pensions and healthcare provision seemed likely to increase. Discuss the effects of this on Japan's future economic growth. [6 marks]

Chapter Ten

Forecasting economic growth

'Forecasting is very difficult, especially if it is about the future.'
Anonymous

Reasons for forecasting economic growth

Forecasts are undertaken by a range of groups. For example, entrepreneurs seek to forecast future demand when they are deciding on what investment to undertake. Speculators also try to assess future prices when considering what to buy and sell.

Politicians ask economists to forecast economic growth so that they can assess the likely affects any given economic growth rate will have on the economy and decide whether they need to adjust their policies and strategies. The Treasury forecast, in particular, informs government policy. For example, if it is forecast that the rate of economic growth will fall below the trend level, a government may decide to adopt reflationary policies. Conversely if it is reported to the Monetary Policy Committee of the Bank of England that the economy is overheating it may decide to raise interest rates.

Forecasters

Economic growth is forecast by a range of groups, including:

- the Treasury
- the Bank of England
- the National Institute of Economic and Social Research (NIESR)
- commercial (high street) banks
- merchant banks (e.g. SBC Warburg, Morgan Stanley)
- academic institutions (e.g. Cambridge Econometrics, Oxford Economic Forecasting)
- international organizations (e.g. the IMF, EU)
- employer organizations (e.g. the CBI)
- Trade unions (e.g. Unison)

Table 10 shows examples of forecasts an compares them with the actual outcome.

Some journalists and academic economists also forecast economic growth. They do this in order to judge the performance of the economy and make recommendations about current and future government policies.

Table 10 Examples of forecasts for economic growth of the UK for 1998

	Growth forecasted (%)
SB Warburg	2.6
NatWest Group	2.3
IMF	2.6
CBI	2.5
Cambridge Econometrics	2.5
NIESR	2.0
HM Treasury	2.5
Barclays Bank	2.6

The outcome was 2.6 per cent growth

Table 11 shows the NIESR forecasts for the economic growth rates for EU member countries for the early part of the twenty-first century.

Table 11 NIESR forecasts for GDP growth (per cent)

	1997	1998	1999	2000	2001–2005
Austria	2.5	3.0	2.3	2.9	2.1
Belgium	3.0	3.0	2.3	2.0	2.4
Denmark	3.1	2.6	1.6	2.1	2.8
Finland	6.0	4.1	2.9	3.5	3.6
France	2.3	3.1	2.4	2.4	2.5
Germany	2.3	2.8	1.8	2.4	2.2
Greece	3.2	3.1	3.1	3.1	3.3
Ireland	9.8	8.9	6.9	6.2	3.4
Italy	1.5	1.6	1.8	2.1	2.6
Netherlands	3.6	3.8	2.1	1.9	2.3
Portugal	3.7	3.8	3.3	3.1	2.9
Spain	3.5	3.8	3.1	2.7	2.4
Sweden	1.8	2.8	2.5	2.2	2.3
UK	**3.5**	**2.5**	**1.0**	**2.5**	**2.2**
EU	2.7	2.9	2.0	2.4	2.4
Euro Area	2.6	2.9	2.2	2.4	2.5

Source: *National Institute Economic Review*, January 1999.

The process of forecasting

There are a number of forecasting methods. The main ones are:

- studying data on, for example, consumer spending, inventory changes, unemployment and investment, to gain information on trends
- examining surveys of, for example, consumer confidence and business investment plans
- studying coincident and leading indicators – see next page
- using **macroeconomic models**.

● Macroeconomic models

Nowadays these are often computer models. They incorporate the information mentioned in the first three methods listed above. They are used to forecast not only economic growth but also other macroeconomic parameters such as unemployment and inflation.

The models include the research findings of the teams that have built them. They build a representation of the economy by using

---

Fears of hard landing start to recede

Gavyn Davies

By the middle of 1998, surveys of business opinion, which had usually proven to be extremely reliable leading indicators for GDP growth, had moved into the extremely depressed territory normally consistent with an outright hard landing. Exports were suffering from a seriously over-valued exchange rate, inventories were rising uncomfortably fast, and consumer confidence was beginning to decline, albeit from extremely high levels.

In the spring of 1999, however, there now seems to be a rising probability that the Treasury's economic forecasts will prove broadly correct, implying that real GDP will fall only moderately below trend during the downswing phase of the economic cycle. Consumer confidence has started to recover, primarily reflecting the monetary policy easing and the continuing healthy performance of the labour market. Equally importantly, there has been some revival in business confidence, though this remains worryingly depressed.

The government has maintained its forecasts for real GDP growth unchanged at 1–1.5 per cent for 1999, and although this remains above the consensus of independent forecasters, there have lately been some indications that the outside consensus is moving upwards towards the government's projection. The chance of an unpleasant hard landing, while certainly not remote, therefore seems to have receded in recent months.

The Independent, 22 March 1999

mathematical equations – in the case of the Treasury model over four hundred of them – which are based on hypotheses about the relationship between economic variables.

For example, a model may postulate that a rise in consumer borrowing will lead to an increase in aggregate demand which in turn will increase output. Economists will estimate what effect, say, a rise of 5 per cent in consumer borrowing will have on GDP. They will then check the actual and projected figures for consumer borrowing and feed them into their model in order to make a forecast.

These models are constantly being updated in the light of new statistical information and developments in economic theory.

Indicators
● Leading indicators
Leading indicators are variables that change usually 2–16 months ahead of the main cycle. The longer leading indicators include surveys of business and consumer confidence and housing starts. Shorter leading indicators include retail sales, new car sales, consumer borrowing and manufacturing orders.

● Coincident indicators
Coincident indicators occur in line with the business cycle and reflect the current state of economic activity. The main coincident indicator is obviously changes in real GDP. Other coincident indicators include changes in the retail price level, and levels of business capacity – although these may occur up to a month after changes in GDP.

● Lagging indicators
Lagging indicators occur after the main changes in economic activity, usually about three months but sometimes up to a year later. They

Forecasters anonymous

David Smith

This may not be healthy, but I keep getting this image of groups of economists sitting around in darkened rooms some time in the future. One by one they stand and, plucking up courage, admit:

'I used to be an economic forecaster.'

The setting-up of Forecasters Anonymous is some way off but, if critics of economics have their way, it could be with us before too long.

The Sunday Times, 14 August 1994

confirm the turning points of the cycle. Unemployment and investment are the best known examples of lagging indicators.

If, for example, there is an upturn in the economy, firms may initially seek to raise output by getting existing workers to work overtime. They will wait some time before they take on new workers to ensure that the higher demand will last.

Difficulties of forecasting

Forecasting is more of an art than a science. As the humorous quote at the start of the chapter indicates, it is not an easy task. Unlike the physical sciences, economists cannot carry out laboratory experiments. It is very difficult to predict human behaviour.

This unpredictability is stressed by Professor Paul Ormerod. He believes that most economists see the economy as a complex machine, one which, if a certain lever is pulled, it can be estimated with some degree of certainty what will happen. He argues that in reality the economy is more complex as it is made up of human beings. He compares it to a living organism whose reactions to any given event are difficult to predict.

A huge number of transactions occur every day. Not all of these can be taken into account in forecasts. The decision as to which ones to include is not easy.

Mistakes can be made in calculating key figures and in interpretation. For example, an economist may estimate the multiplier incorrectly or may interpret a fall in private sector spending to be a short-term change which will be self-correcting whereas it may actually be the start of a recession.

In addition, however good the models are their predictions can be thrown off line by unforeseen events and time lags. As with weather forecasts, the further ahead forecasts of economic growth are made, the less reliable they tend to be.

The evidence analysed may also send out conflicting signals. For instance, what is to be made of a situation where surveys indicate that consumer confidence is low but retail sales are seen to rise?

Technically no recession

- Technically, our central forecast suggests that recession is avoided. A recession is defined by most economists as at least two quarters of negative growth. On this definition, our forecast shows no recession, although the next four or five quarters are likely to see rather anaemic growth.
- Our model of the economy suggests that next year's growth rate is very sensitive to small changes in interest rates or exchange rates. As a result, the downturn could easily turn into recession if the Bank keeps interest rates too high for too long. This sensitivity means that the margin of error around our central growth forecast is correspondingly large.
- The outlook for the economy also depends crucially on confidence, which is extremely hard to predict.
- If large enough, share price falls could damage economic growth in the industrialized world. Simulations on the OECD world economic model suggest that a sustained 20 per cent price decline would cut GDP in the industrialized world by 0.4 per cent by the end of the second year.
- We have done some simulations on our model of even larger falls in share prices (e.g. around 50 per cent price decline). The main message of these simulations is that, even with much larger price declines, recession is avoided in all major industrialized countries (with the exception of Japan – which is already in recession).

Source: Extracts from Lloyds Bank *Economic Bulletin*, October 1998

KEY WORDS

Forecasting	Coincident indicators
Macroeconomic models	Lagging indicators
Leading indicators	

Further reading

Mackintosh, M. *et al.*, Chapter 2 in *Economics and Changing Economies*, Open University Press, 1996.

Ormerod, P., Chapters 4 and 5 in *The Death of Economics*, Faber & Faber, 1994.

Smith, D., Chapter 4 in *UK Current Economic Policy*, 2nd edn, Heinemann Educational, 1999.

'The Economist', Chapter 4 in *Guide to Economic Indicators*, 3rd edn, *The Economist*/Profile Books.

Useful websites
Oxford Economic Forecasting: www.oxecon.co.uk/
OECD: www.oecd.org/std/index.htm

Essay topics
1. (a) Explain the various factors an economist is likely to consider when trying to forecast the level of aggregate investment. [12 marks]
   (b) Discuss the impact of investment expenditure upon employment and economic growth. [13 marks] {Associated Examining Board 1997]
2. Assess how useful economic forecasts are in assisting the formation of economic policy. [25 marks]

Data response question
Read the following article from the NIESR's *National Institute Economic Review* of January 1999, and study the chart. Then answer the questions that follow.

The US should expand by 2.2 per cent in 1999, helped by the substantial decline in oil prices which has a strong effect on the energy intensive American economy. Crude oil is now expected to fetch $12 per barrel in 1999, almost a quarter lower than seemed likely at the time of our last forecast. Simulations on our model suggest that this sharp decline in oil prices will raise US growth by 0.5 percentage points while reducing consumer price inflation by 0.5 to 0.75 percentage points, more than offsetting any inflationary impulse from the recent fall in the dollar.

With the yen appreciating and long-run interest rates rising sharply, the outlook for the Japanese economy remains bleak. Despite the boost from new fiscal measures, output will fall by 0.5 per cent a year, and consumer prices will decline by nearly 1 per cent, pushing up real interest rates commensurately. The scope for further fiscal expansion is limited by the budget deficit already running at 8 per cent of GDP over the next two fiscal years. The government urgently needs to announce a plan to inject more money into the economy, generating expectations of higher inflation and bringing down the yen.

Economic growth in the Euro Area is now expected to fall from almost 3 per cent in 1998 to 2.2 per cent in 1999.

Figure A   OEDC GDP growth (per cent)

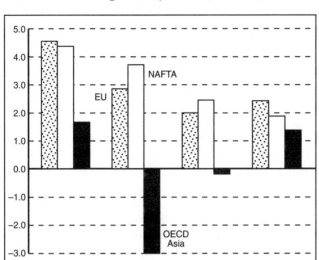

1. Describe the changes in economic growth shown in the graph. [4 marks]
2. Explain what is meant by an economic model. [3 marks]
3. What effect would a rise in oil prices have on the NIESR's prediction for NAFTA growth rates in 1999 and 2000? [5 marks]
4. Explain how 'generating expectations of higher inflation and bringing down the yen' could generate economic growth in Japan. [7 marks]
5. On the basis of what information might the NIESR have predicted a fall in the growth rate of the Euro Area? [6 marks]

Conclusion

This book has sought to examine the nature, causes and effects of economic growth and fluctuations in economic growth. In discussing the causes of economic growth, the key role of investment in being able to increase both aggregate demand and supply was identified.

It was also concluded that, whilst care has to be taken to avoid the costs of economic growth, most countries, both developed and developing, believe that the benefits of economic growth exceed the cost.

The challenges facing developing and developed countries vary to a certain extent in that the main problem still facing many developing countries is how to achieve economic growth (and alter the structure of their output and employment) whereas the main problem facing developed countries is how to manage their economic growth. However, an increasing awareness is being shown in both types of economies of the desirability of sustainable growth.

Government measures, including recent UK government policy measures, and differences in policy approaches between Keynesian and new classical economists were discussed.

The relationship between economic growth and some key markets was explored. This discussion again brought out the benefits and possible risks of economic growth, the need for economic growth to be sustainable and the important roles that certain variables including education, health and technology play in determining economic growth.

In examining business cycles it was concluded that these remain a real risk. This view was reinforced by the discussion of the recent global crisis which has shown how vulnerable the world still is to fluctuations in economic activity.

Economic growth can improve peoples' lives, especially if it is of a stable and sustainable nature. However, as this book has sought to show, there are a number of important, interesting and valuable challenges connected with economic growth. These include

- identifying the key determinant or determinants of growth
- deciding on which policies are most effective in promoting sustainable economic growth, and
- eliminating business cycles and developing more reliable economic forecasting models.

Index